ROYAL YACHTS OF EUROPE

ROYAL YACHTS OF EUROPE

From the Seventeenth to Twentieth Century

REGINALD CRABTREE

DAVID & CHARLES

NEWTON ABBOT LONDON VANCOUVER

ISBN 0 7153 6754 4

Set in 11 on 13pt Imprint by
Wordsworth Typesetting London
and printed in Great Britain
by Biddles Limited Guildford
for David & Charles (Holdings) Limited
South Devon House Newton Abbot Devon

Published in Canada
by Douglas David & Charles Limited
132 Philip Avenue North Vancouver BC

CONTENTS

INTRODUCTION

Vessels of rare distinction and fabulous construction, built for the conveyance of great personages on state or pleasure ventures, or during naval campaigns, made their first appearance in the ancient empires of the Mediterranean. The Greek and Roman galleys, the Nile barges of the pharaohs, which carried the legendary figures of antiquity, were all essentially propelled by oars, although, with a favourable following wind, a single square sail could be hoisted in most cases, and used to advantage.

The royal ships of medieval Europe, resplendent with gilded carving and purple silk, reflecting the might and wealth of kings were, more often than not, barely comfortable for anything but the shortest of sea voyages, and almost totally at the mercy of wind and tide. Seafaring was a notoriously dangerous procedure, and royal journeys by sea were limited to those of utter necessity. There was little or no pleasure cruising indulged in by kings or their subjects in Europe before the seventeenth century, despite the splendid outward appearance of some royal ships.

It was the Dutch burghers of the State of Holland in the seventeenth-century Republic of the Netherlands, who first conceived the idea that to sail small, elaborately fitted and decorated vessels could be pleasurable – and prestigious. The way in which a Stuart prince, who, in exile became keen on sailing such *jaghts*, and in returning to England as Charles II to restore the monarchy, brought with him the Dutch *jaght – Mary –* is well known as the starting point of what came to be known universally as 'yachting'. The 'Merry Monarch' is rightly acclaimed as the father of both the sport and pastime as it developed beyond the original Dutch 'boat pageantry', and gradually spread – at first entirely for royal participation – throughout Europe.

As was to be expected, the royal yachting of Charles II was emulated by the English nobility, and from then onwards yachting was seeded in two beds, taking root in royal and popular soil, and each basic stem produced its counterparts in Europe generally. Just as the economic and social climate in Holland had produced the idea of the yacht, English shipbuilding skill and the personal enthusiasm of the king, saw the Dutch ideas modified and steadily improved, until English yachts reached a standard of excellence, in sea-keeping qualities and handiness, with accommodation which was both comfortable and ornately decorative.

Such royal yachts grew in size and magnificence from the Stuarts to the Hanoverians, and a similar precedence for the use of an official yacht was reflected in many of the royal courts of Europe. This was something quite different from the former use of royal ships, and largely because of the improved design and build of ships stemming from English yards, it became possible to equip such vessels in a manner which not only provided comfort, but also reflected a grandeur and style of living to which monarchs were then accustomed. By the eighteenth century the royal yacht had become as much a part of the expected accoutrement of monarchy as were the numerous country houses to which European royalty retired for pleasurable relaxation. In many cases royal yachts were as well appointed, but there was also a strictly official side in their use for state occasions and the conveyance of ambassadors and important visitors. In almost all cases they were maintained by the national navy, and could be used, if the occasion arose, as despatch vessels.

The Age of Reason which produced the

neo-classical forms of eighteenth-century architecture was reflected in ship, and particularly royal yacht, decoration and fittings, not surprisingly, since the artists and craftsmen who were employed also served the house builders. Modifications, which might be termed 'Dutch yacht baroque', and 'British marine classical', continued to be used, particularly in yachts, into the nineteenth century, and because wood panelling became an accepted part of yacht interiors, it has remained part of a maritime tradition in interior decoration.

The figure-head of a ship has a mystic significance lying deep in the ancient mythology of the sea, and it remained, until recent times, the essential finish to the bow decoration of a yacht. This aspect of marine art is a study in itself but it is sufficient to say here that, by the turn of the eighteenth century, it had reached a highly stylised form in royal yachts. Kings, queens, gods and goddesses, highly painted and gilded, and anatomically adapted to fit the bow to which they were attached, stared rigidly ahead from beneath the bowsprit. The elaborate scroll work, or 'gingerbread' which was also a part of the bow decoration, evolved from Dutch and English patterns, and strangely enough, even today it cannot be modernised without losing some essential yacht quality.

Gingerbread decoration was continued down the sides with 'wreaths' round gunports (used for saluting-guns only) ending in a spectacular design at the stern. In yachts with built up poopdeck sterns and windowed galleries surmounted with lanterns, the decoration also managed to include the royal coat of arms amid highly gilded and painted baroque swirls, twists and filigree work, creating a splendid effect overall.

The development of the steam engine virtually banished the royal sailing yacht from its official role, and thereafter it remained to fulfil the more informal side of royal yachting – sail racing. From about the 1830s, first the paddle-wheel yacht and then the screw schooner, took their respective places as desirable forms of official royal yachts throughout Europe. There now began a period which lasted until World War I, in which some of the greatest steam yachts ever built held the forefront of attention, and it seemed as if there was no limit to which some monarchs would go to have the biggest and most sumptuous of this new and exciting form of private sea-transport. British shipbuilders had pioneered the steam yacht, and as in the case of the sporting sail yacht, a large proportion of Europe's royal yachts originally came off the stocks of Scottish yards. But in time there were some notable examples from some European builders.

By the end of the nineteenth century the steam yacht – developing through a period of sail and steam – was in its most attractive form, the screw schooner. It was now possible to have a yacht which was completely independent of the vagaries of wind and tide, with accommodation in a style similarly palatial to a royal dwelling ashore. Furthermore, the ladies – who had been somewhat deterred by the more rigorous conditions under sail – found steam yachting very much to their liking. The power that had been wielded behind the throne at country house parties was able to play its part at similar occasions aboard steam yachts.

Everything was done to provide these royal vessels with interiors which reflected the status of the monarch. It has been said that the problem which confronted the yacht architect at this time was how to put a palace into a mobile steel tank. Judging from the big steam yachts of the period there is little doubt that they succeeded handsomely. But there was one important aspect other than outward show, in which all royal yachts shared – they provided an element of sanctuary for monarchs and their families, not found as completely in any other of their establishments. With a picked company of officers and men – not difficult to recruit with the better living conditions of royal yacht service – royalty could relax and share for a while the simple pleasures of a family life, all but denied them ashore. Royal yacht crews were looked upon as devoted family servants, particularly by the Imperial Russian family.

Such yachts also made possible the visits to regattas in the Baltic, Mediterranean, or British waters, where, almost amid an exclusive 'royal club' gathering, the more informal sport of yacht racing could be indulged. To cater for this kind of relaxation, many yacht clubs, under royal patronage, were well established by the end of the nineteenth century. From the Black Sea to the Baltic they all in general followed the lead of Britain's Royal Yacht Squadron – exclusive and dedicated to a kind of Corinthian ideal.

The ensuing pages contain a representative selection of royal yachts of European countries which have been, or are still, monarchies, and ranging from the seventeenth century to the present day, have served as either formal marine homes or as sporting craft. The word 'yacht' escapes exact definition, but broadly it must be contained within such strictures which describe a vessel used for pleasure in sport or pastime, not primarily a warship and propelled otherwise than by oars. One vessel, not strictly a yacht under these terms, is included – *Le Canot Impérial* of Napoleon Bonaparte. This has been described because, besides its obvious interest, it is an example of a type of royal vessel of limited use which has appeared concurrently with official yachts throughout European history.

Royal yachting meant for its participants a welcome escape from the cares of the crown, and for that reason the sources of information about cruises and informal occasions are understandably unrevealing. Log books, when available, give little more than the bald facts of navigation. So far as is known, there are but three national works on royal yachts – British, Danish and Dutch.* Where only partial statistics about yachts were available, estimates from comparisons with vessels of similar size and build have been made. Similarly for the drawings and reconstructions reference has been made to whatever contemporary material was available.

Royal Europe of the kind that existed intact until 1914, in which fortunes were spent by some monarchs at the merest whim, has disappeared completely. The results of the expenditure of vast amounts, lavishly, and often recklessly undertaken by Europe's royal houses in the past, has had, at least, the effect of leaving for posterity great works of art and architecture which can still be seen and enjoyed. In the case of the big yachts which were kept in constant commission as a recognised adjunct to royal places ashore, and which were in themselves works of art, they have disappeared almost entirely – in a great number of cases without trace. The breaker's yard cares nothing for fine craftsmanship.

The illustrations which follow are a reminder that there existed yachts which have assumed over the years a character which is inherent in the best ship design. Underlying such quality and style is the too often forgotten ingenuity and craft-skill of countless men and women, all over the continent, who by their labours produced the splendour and panache of almost three centuries of royal yachts of Europe.

* C. M. Gavin, *Royal Yachts* (Rich & Cowan), 1932; R. Steen Steensen, *De Danske Kongers Skibe* (Copenhagen, 1972); G. W. E. Crone, *De Jachten Der Oranjes* (Amsterdam, 1937).

AUSTRIA-HUNGARY

Fantasie

paddle-yacht

Built by Samuda Bros of Poplar, London in 1857. Loa 176ft, beam 16ft, draught 9ft. Iron hull rigged with two masts. TM tonnage: 330. Engines: simple oscillating steam of 400hp, giving 13 knots.

The treaty of Utrecht in 1713 removed the possibility of Austrian domination of Spain, but the Habsburgs still ruled as latter-day emperors of much of what was left of the Holy Roman Empire, and remained a powerful influence in Europe. It was not until the nineteenth century that the complex problems of Austrian hegemony began to obtrude in a way which finally led to World War I. During most of that time the long lived Emperor Franz Joseph held together rather tenuously the Dual Monarchy of Austria-Hungary, ruling from Vienna, and a competent Imperial Navy was built and fitted out in the Adriatic.

As in other European nations, the paddle-yacht became a necessary adjunct for royal use in Austria in the 1850s, and Franz Joseph's first official imperial yacht was the *Fantasie*. She would have been fitted out comfortably and expensively in a German style rather than Hungarian, much like the admiral's quarters of a warship.

There is little known about *Fantasie*'s movements, but it seems likely that she was

used almost exclusively on the Danube, with perhaps appearances at Pola and Venice on the occasions of imperial state visits, or for fleet reviews. What is certainly known is that Emperor Franz Joseph was present at the opening of the Suez Canal in 1869, and it seems entirely likely that the imperial Austrian yacht which featured in the report of the proceedings was the *Fantasie*.

This well built but somewhat unassuming imperial yacht was on the establishment of the Imperial and Royal Navy until replaced by the larger *Miramar* in 1872. She was then relegated to use as a hulk, and was finally struck off the fleet list during World War I.

The rather solitary soldierly figure of the longest reigning monarch in Europe, does not readily suggest that Franz Joseph used his imperial yachts for any extended pleasure cruising. His concern to continue what he saw as the sacred trust of the Habsburgs, together with the domination of his household by his mother, the Dowager Empress Sophie, were factors which made life at court impossible for his young, inexperienced Empress Elizabeth. It is more than likely that it was she who may have used the imperial yachts in an effort to find relaxation.

Miramar   paddle-yacht

Built by Samuda Bros London in 1872. Loa 269ft, beam 32·8ft, draught 14ft. Iron hull rigged as a schooner. TM tonnage: 1,830. Engines: direct acting steam of 2,500ihp, giving 17·2 knots. Bunker capacity: 300 tons.

Miramar is an excellent example of the work of the firm of Samuda Bros of London, who produced a large number of ships, and were particularly known for their fine paddle-yachts, which were built on the Thames at a time – from the early decades of the nineteenth century – when there was much shipbuilding activity on the London river. She was built expressly for HIM Franz Joseph, Emperor of Austria, and represents a kind of second stage in the development of the paddle-yacht. A comparison with *Fantasie*, which is in the earlier, or first stage and is more fundamental in design, shows *Miramar* to be a much more elegant yacht, with her paddle-boxes, and funnels fitting into a better overall conception. The gunport portholes on the main deck level are features of most royal paddle-yachts of this period.

Fashion, which played such a part in the social lives of kings and courtiers in Europe, was no less a factor in the kind of yachts which were produced for royalty once steam yachts had firmly ousted sail in the latter half of the nineteenth century. *Miramar* was in all respects a suitable yacht for her imperial and royal master. It is most likely that her interior arrangements and decoration were in a similar style to those of *Fantasie*, although she would have had greater space and amenities.

The Habsburg family, led by the autocratic Franz Joseph as emperor and king of the Dual Monarchy of the Austro-Hungarian Empire, was numerous. The highly dramatic personal tragedies which depleted the line of succession, and which finally brought Archduke Charles to the tottering imperial throne, are well known. In a wealth of documentation there is little or no reference to the part official yachts played. It can be surmised that they were used as a means of getting away from officialdom.

The Austro-Hungarian Navy had on its establishment other yachts beside the three royal official ones. *Taurus* is mentioned as bearing Prince Wilhelm zu Wied to his short-lived reign as King of Albania. *Miramar* was armed with two 14-pounders and may have been used as a naval auxiliary. The fashionable side of yachting seems to have flourished mainly in the Hungarian side of the empire, as will be seen from what follows.

Built by Ramage & Ferguson Ltd at Leith in 1911, for HIH the Archduke Charles Stephen of Austria. Loa 186·5ft, beam 29·1ft, draught 16·1ft. Steel hull rigged with two masts. TM tonnage: 709. Engines: triple-expansion 3-cylinder steam, fed by two boilers giving 138nhp; built by Ramage & Fergusons.

The Imperial and Royal Austro-Hungarian Navy listed only three official royal yachts on their establishment. They were the paddle-wheelers *Fantasie* and *Miramar*, already mentioned, and both London built, and the *Greif*, built at Pola in 1885. This latter yacht was somewhat smaller than the *Miramar* – being 73m, loa, and of 1,370 TM tons, compared to 82m and 1,830 TM tons. Both of them were handed over to Italy as war reparations in 1920.

In the Hungarian Kingdom of the Dual Monarchy, from the start of the fashionable yachting period until the outbreak of hostilities in 1914, there had grown a strong yachting tradition among the Habsburg nobility, and one man in particular – Archduke Charles Stephen – was a great enthusiast. In 1884, the Stefania Yacht Club had been founded with Crown Princess Stefania as Patron, and Graf M.Esterhazy as Commodore, and it is likely that the Archduke was a member; but by 1891 the Austro-Hungarian Imperial and Royal Yacht Squadron was established at Pola with a very impressive list of members. Under the patronage of the Emperor, Archduke Stephen was Commodore, and the Vice-Commodores included the Prince of Lichtenstein, Duke Philip of Saxe-Coburg-Gotha, and Prince Bathyany-Strattman.

Archduke Stephen owned many yachts but the best known was the *Ul*, built for him in 1911. She was a fine steam yacht of the period, with excellent and splendidly fitted accommodation on two decks and a promenade deck, with electric lighting throughout. In her the Archduke made many cruises, but he was also a competent and active sailing yachtsman, the possessor of a Yacht Master's Certificate, and he was a friend of King Edward VII, who sponsored his membership of the Royal Thames Yacht Club. The name *Ul* – which means 'Hive' – was given to his steam yacht because, he is reported to have said that, with his large family, the yacht was like a bee hive when they were all on board.

During World War I, *Ul* was captured by Italian forces at Trieste, but the timely intervention of the King of Spain enabled her owner to retain her. After the war, the Archduke sold her to the American millionaire A. J. Drexel, who renamed her *Sayonara*.

BELGIUM

Alberta

twin-screw schooner

Built by Ailsa Shipbuilding & Engineering Co, from designs by G. L. Watson, at Troon, Scotland in 1896. Loa 252·6ft, beam 33·7ft, draught 15·4ft. Steel hull rigged with two masts. TM tonnage: 1,322. Engines: two quadruple-expansion 8-cylinder steam, fed by two Scotch boilers, giving 448nhp, and speed of 17 knots; built by D. Rowan & Son, Glasgow.

The Saxe-Coburg line of Belgium's monarchs starts from 1831 when the country finally emerged as an independent kingdom. Her first king – Leopold I – used the impressive state barge *Le Canot du Roi*, which had been specially built for him and his family, on suitable occasions; but, with one notable exception, Belgian kings have not used yachts.

Leopold II, succeeding his father in 1865, was an exception to almost everything connected with monarchy. He ruled for forty-four years and in that time his activities in the world of commerce amassed for him a personal fortune, and finally saddled Belgium with his notorious slave-labour money-maker, the Belgian Congo. He had a particularly keen interest in shipping lines, and the interior decoration of the Ostend-Dover ships received

his personal supervision. Congo wood and ivory were much in evidence in the saloons and restaurants of these ships in the 1890s.

About 1899, he acquired the steam yacht *Alberta* (she was originally named *Margarita* and built for US millionaire A. J. Drexel), and from what can be gleaned through the secrecy which surrounded all Leopold's activities, it seems that he was fond of yachting – of a kind. *Alberta* was always registered in the name of his agents – Little & Johnson. At Cap Ferrat, in the South of France, in which country the king spent a great deal of time, he founded a fashionable suburb, and a harbour for *Alberta*, where this fine yacht lay at permanent moorings. Leopold used her magnificent accommodation, particularly the library at the forward end of the deckhouses, as a business office. At the end of each day he would go ashore, be helped onto a motor-tricycle – which he called 'mon animal' – and thence drive off to his mistress, Caroline Lacroix, at the Villa des Cedres.

The 'Tycoon King' never used *Alberta* for official royal occasions, but after his death in 1909, she had a most varied and useful life; first as *Rozsviet* in the Russian Navy in 1918, and then as HMS *Surprise* in the British Navy in the two World Wars. She was still listed as a yacht in 1950.

GREAT BRITAIN

Fubbs

Built by Phineas Pett at Greenwich in 1682, for King Charles II. Loa 80ft, beam 21ft, 148 tons burden. Large sail area, which gave her exceptional speed, suggested by the fact of her substantial mainmast of 22in 'Norway stick'.

King Charles II not only restored the monarchy to England in 1660, but his knowledge of maritime affairs boosted naval development and scientific discovery; and his personal keenness for sailing, together with the arrival of the Dutch *jaght* – *Mary* – a parting gift from Amsterdam, started what has continued to grow in Europe, the sport and pastime of yachting. Quite soon a receptive and well developed shipbuilding trade was modifying the Dutch prototype *jaght* in the sharper bows, deeper draught and straight keel minus lee boards, of the English yacht.

Up to 1685, some twenty yachts were built for the king, mostly by the talented Pett family. They were used for racing (particularly the *Jamie*, 25 tons, and the *Bezan*, 35 tons) – an innovation which has rightly earned for Charles II the title of 'the Father of Yachting' – and for the pleasure cruising, about which occupation, Pepys and Evelyn have left much comment. *Fubbs* – so named after the King's nickname for the Duchess of Portsmouth, and colloquially then meaning plump or chubby – was the first and finest of the two-masted ship or ketch which Charles II is said to have invented as a suitable yacht rig. Two masts, main and mizzen, carried square topsails with loose-footed fore and aft sails; the mizzen sail in early ketches like *Fubbs*, has a long lateen yard which later became the gaff of a leg-of-mutton shaped sail. The rig of smaller yachts of the period was of the 'smack cutter' type, with loose-footed mainsail, long gaff (or half 'spreet'), and two headsails with the possibility of a square topsail.

Showing none of the qualities suggested by her name, *Fubbs* proved an exceptionally fine yacht, having sailing abilities which surpassed any other, and a remarkable turn of speed. Her exterior decoration followed closely the practices discussed earlier (p.8). The royal cabin, situated aft, and entered from a richly decorated ante room, was panelled in carved oak, with an inlaid floor, and included a great four-poster bed resplendent with gold brocades and silks.

This most excellent royal yacht continued in service until 1781, although, in accordance with contemporary practices, she had virtually been rebuilt several times, but retained the name of *Fubbs* on each occasion.

Built in Deptford for HRH The Prince of Wales (later King George IV) in 1817. Loa 103ft (gundeck), beam 26·5ft, depth in hold 11·5ft. Rigged as a three-masted ship, classed as a 'second rater', of 330 tons burden. Originally carried eight brass 1-pounder swivel saluting-guns.

The precedents for royal yachts, created by Charles II, continued through the successive reigns of James II, William and Mary, Anne, and the Hanoverians, but with never again the same number of yachts built for any one monarch, and not until the late nineteenth century would royal yachts again be raced. In the Hanoverian period, several vessels were built which variously served as royal yachts, of which two were outstanding.

By all accounts the *Royal Sovereign* of 1804 was magnificently fitted out. Ship-rigged and built at Deptford, she was used often by George III, on many occasions for cruises to his favourite resort of Weymouth; but the yacht which caught the public eye was the *Royal George*. Deservedly famous, not only for her sailing qualities, but for a number of unique attributes; she was designed to suit the personal convenience of 'Prinny'; had Nelson's old captain, Sir Edward Berry, as her first commander; and when broken up in 1905, she was the oldest royal yacht in the world, and the third oldest ship in the Royal Navy.

In 1902, when moved from her moorings as an accommodation hulk for officers and men of the royal yachts in Portsmouth, the *Daily*

Graphic, of 11 April, gave her an obituary spread which would have done justice to a monarch. But while in commission she had her moments of popular interest and acclaim. The illustration shows how she would have appeared when she lay off Brighton for the Prince Regent's first cruise in her.

Great crowds had assembled for the occasion, and having inspected the newly built Royal Pavilion, designed by John Nash, the Prince went out to the *Royal George*, and on board there followed a house warming party of some magnitude. When finally the royal yacht put to sea, the weather proved too inclement for the tender state of her passengers

and she returned to Brighton within hours! Some contemporary 'Corinthian' wag has left a neo-heroic poem: 'Address to the *Royal George* Yacht', the gist of which is given by the first and last couplets:

> Hail, gaudy Ship, what wonders hast
> thou done,
> To tempt to Sea our Monarch's eldest
> son!
> ..   ..
> To keep the Sea at such a time were
> vain –
> You therefore brought the Regent
> back again.

Victoria and Albert I-III

(I) Paddle-yacht, loa 225ft, beam 33ft, draught 14ft. Wooden hull, 1,034 tons burden. One mast and auxiliary sails. Engines: Maudslay's 2-cylinder 'Siamese' steam; 785ihp. (II) Paddle-yacht, loa 329ft, beam 40·3ft, draught 16·3ft. Wooden hull, 2,470 tons displacement. Three masts. Engines: Penn & Sons 2-cylinder oscillating steam; 2,400ihp. (III) Twin-screw schooner, loa 430ft, beam 50ft, draught 17ft. Steel hull with teak sheath. TM tonnage: 5,000. Three masts. Engines: two triple-expansion steam; 11,800bhp. All three yachts built at Pembroke to Admiralty designs.

King George IV, as the Prince Regent became, did use the *Royal George* on many occasions, and his membership of what became the Royal Yacht Squadron is well known, but he was the last monarch to use official sailing yachts. Queen Victoria after one trip in the *Royal George* thereafter had steam yachts.

An interest in yachting, gained from early cruises in the Solent with her mother, and the happy co-operation of Prince Albert, meant that during her reign Queen Victoria had some six steam yachts built. The three largest – all named *Victoria and Albert* – were constantly

used. But it was the second of that name which the queen favoured most. She retained it to the last, disliking the great new royal yacht, and never using it.

Paddle-yacht *Victoria and Albert II* has in some ways become a symbol of all that Victorian yachting meant, epitomised by Cowes Week Regatta, which grew from simple beginnings into a royal occasion even for many European monarchs. The simple delight which the queen found in Osborne House – rebuilt as an Italianate demi-palace under Prince Albert's instructions – and the Prince of Wales' keenness for yacht racing, made it an essential function of the court's year.

Victoria and Albert II not only lay at Cowes, but in her the Queen and Prince Albert made many visits, particularly to out of the way parts of Britain, and thus enhanced her popularity with thousands of her subjects. There is much evidence that this yacht was often in use not only by the queen, but was also made available to royal visitors. In the latter years of her reign, when the queen remained almost a recluse at Osborne, and

BUILT FOR HER BRITANNIC MAJESTY
QUEEN VICTORIA

Paddle-wheel Yacht - VICTORIA and ALBERT I - 1843

Paddle-wheel Yacht - VICTORIA and ALBERT II - 1855

Twin-Screw Yacht - VICTORIA and ALBERT III - 1899

when there was a continual coming and going of her ministers, the smaller royal yachts, *Elfin*, *Alberta* and *Osborne*, came into their own as ferry-boats! These three paddle-yachts, and the screw yacht *Fairy* had been used as tenders to the bigger yachts, but it was to *Alberta* that fell the sad honour of carrying the mortal remains of the queen from her beloved Isle of Wight.

Victoria and Albert III

the drawing-room

Because of an accident which occurred in dry dock, due to miscalculations in her weight distributions, which delayed her commissioning until the year of Queen Victoria's death, and combined with the fact that the queen had taken a dislike to the yacht, the third *Victoria and Albert* became the official royal yacht of King Edward VII. Although the king had the smaller twin-screw turbine yacht *Alexandra* built, she was only used as a cross-channel ferry, and *Victoria and Albert III* was then the biggest and most magnificent royal yacht in Europe.

This impressive steam yacht became very much part of official royal occasions in Europe and at home. From the Mediterranean to the Baltic she steamed thousands of miles, and appeared at many regattas. Serving three monarchs, she carried King George V and Queen Mary at the Jubilee Review of 1935,

and made her last appearance before being withdrawn from service, in 1937, at the Coronation Review, carrying King George VI and his queen.

Something has been said earlier about traditional ideas regarding the interior decoration of yachts, and from the first to the last of the *Victoria and Albert*s, there was a distinct move away from the style which had so enhanced the interiors of *Royal Sovereign* and the *Royal George* with the elegant, traditional wood carving, gilded and damask-covered panelling of the royal apartments. Looking at the illustration of the interior of *Victoria and Albert III*, one might be looking at the drawing-room of the best of the English country houses of the 1900s. In steam yachts certainly there was opportunity to follow current decoration and furnishing of the mansion ashore. Although the popular 'Gothick' style did find its way into some yacht interiors – particularly in the profusion of ornaments and brice-a-brac – the Victorian royal yachts reflect a simplicity of taste, certainly not lacking in elegance which in large measure was due to Queen Victoria's dislike, perhaps fostered by Prince Albert, of the regal splendour of past monarchs. The last two *Victoria and Albert*s are both distinctly royal homes. The second of the yachts, with its chintzes, mahogany furniture and Brussels carpets was indeed homely.

Victoria and Albert III represents the last great steam yacht in pre-1914 royal Europe – a long way from the 'neatness and room in so small a vessel' which Samuel Pepys so admired in the first English royal yacht, the *Mary*.

Britannia

cutter

Built by D & W Henderson & Co of Glasgow, in April 1893, to designs of G. L. Watson, for HRH The Prince of Wales (later King Edward VII). Loa 100ft, lwl 87.87ft, beam 23.3ft, draught 12.6ft. TM tonnage: 221. Hull of composite construction. Original rig: gaff-topsail cutter. Sail area: 10,359.1 sq ft. Sails by Ratsey & Lapthorn.

The building of *Britannia* to G. L. Watson's design marked a new era in yacht racing, with the new conception of a yacht that skimmed over the waves rather than the 'plank on edge' yacht which ploughed through them. She was faster to windward in light airs, and twice as fast in strong ones. The Prince of Wales delighted in this beautiful yacht, as did all yachtsmen who saw her or raced against her. She became almost a personality. From the Clyde to Cannes, she swept the board of racing trophies in her first years; then, due to unpleasantness caused by the German Kaiser, *Britannia* was sold out of royal ownership, and with cut down rig she became a cruising yacht.

Bought back by Edward VII, and recommissioned for racing in 1920 by George V, it was Britain's 'Sailor King' who so cherished this magnificent yacht, and who proved in many races that his *Britannia* had lost none of her fine qualities. With her rig changed to the new 'Bermudian', and with King George V at her helm, *Britannia* epitomises the last days of the great J Class yachts. It was thus a fitting end when at his death the king's wishes were carried out and on 10 July 1936, witnessed by her old crew members, *Britannia*, under the direction of HMS *Amazon* and HMS *Winchelsea*, was sunk off St Catherine's Point Lighthouse. Since then she has remained a splendid legend in the hearts of yachtsmen throughout Europe.

Britannia

Built by John Brown Ltd, on the Clyde in 1954, to Admiralty designs. Loa 412·2ft, beam 55ft, draught 15·6ft. Steel hull, rigged with three masts. TM tonnage: 5,111. Engines: two *geared steam turbines fed by two water-tube boilers – oil fired, giving 12,000 bhp, and a speed of 22·75 knots. Fitted with roll-stabilisers.*

Coweslip

Built and designed by Uffa Fox at Cowes in 1947. Loa 20ft, beam 5ft, draught (ex-centre board) 2·5ft, Sail area : 150 sq ft.

The greatest and smallest of royal yachts together in one photograph summarises British royal yachting in the present era. Steam yacht *Britannia* is the biggest official royal yacht in Europe today, and appropriately she is a fine example of Clydeside shipbuilding expertise, retaining Britain's past traditions. In keeping with modern democratic attitudes, her construction allows for her speedy conversion to a hospital ship of the Royal Navy, should occasion require it.

Since her commissioning, *Britannia* has been used for royal visits to all parts of the Commonwealth, and such state duties do not allow HM the Queen and her family to be regular visitors to Cowes Regatta Week, although HRH Prince Philip is Admiral of the Royal Yacht Squadron. However, when *Britannia* is there, the royal presence, and the magnificent sight of the yacht's immaculate dark blue hull with white upperworks, produces a heightened quality about the occasion. The royal apartments in this great yacht are aft on the upper and shelter decks, with an observation bridge at the forward end of the latter. Furnishing and decor, in a modern idiom, reflect the elegant simplicity of earlier royal yachts.

Coweslip (a contraction of 'Cowes' and 'Slip', from whence she came) a wedding gift from the people of Cowes, like the 29ft Dragon *Bluebottle* – given by the Island Sailing Club – and the older *Bloodhound* (now as a yawl, available on loan to encourage sail cruising) have all given Prince Philip a chance to show his skill and enthusiasm for sailing. He has by his example done much to encourage the sport.

HRH Prince Philip at the tiller, tacking *Coweslip* down past *Britannia,* with the late Uffa Fox as crew – both dressed in seaman's oilskins – echoes, in a more informal way, precedents set three centuries before by Charles II, who, we are told by Pepys, 'handled the sails like a common seaman'.

BULGARIA

Nadiejda

*Built in Bordeaux, France, in 1898. Loa 200ft
(est), beam 23ft (est), draught 12·5ft. Gross
tonnage : 715. Steel hull, rigged with two masts.
Engines : Two sets triple-expansion steam, fed by
French built water-tube boilers (est), driving
twin-screws and giving 17 knots.*

Balkan history is so complex, so intricately
woven into the main fabric of Europe, that it
defies easy, or brief summary. Bulgaria, gaining
independence from Turkish domination in
1908, became something of an enigma to the
rest of Europe, but at least she showed a
degree of national loyalty which was lacking in
other Balkan kingdoms, and she remained a
monarchy until the iron curtain of Communist
rule was drawn across much of the Balkans
after World War II.

Following his father, the liberator King
Ferdinand, King Boris III ruled Bulgaria
until 1943. It is difficult to assess the importance which Bulgaria placed on royal yachts,
but like most of Europe's monarchs who were
keen Francophiles, Boris and his family would
have taken part in the coming and going at
French Riveria resorts, probably in chartered
yachts, in the seasons between the wars.
However, there are two vessels which have
been listed as royal yachts.

Bulgaria's marine littoral, like that of her
neighbours, is the shallow Black Sea, and the
ancient mother of European trade – the great
River Danube. It is likely that the elderly
paddle-yacht *Kroum* – similar in size and
functional design to the Yugoslavian *Dragor*
(see p92) was used on the Danube
exclusively.

Nadiejda with her ram type bow was built
at a time when builders and designers of the
important torpedo boats, and their antidotes
the torpedo boat destroyers – or just destroyers
as they were finally called – were involved in
an increasing competition, in which every extra
knot of speed counted. Used as a Bulgarian
royal yacht, she was certainly modified for
extra accommodation, and the deckhouse
which can be seen built up aft, was probably
similar in function to the kind of pavilion
saloon erected aft in a number of European
royal yachts in the nineteenth century. It
might also have served as a dining saloon or
lounge. The royal yacht *Nadiejda* could have
been used either from Black Sea ports or on
the Danube, and, according to Brassy's
Naval Annual of 1912, apart from *Nadiejda*
there were some ten small steamers which
comprised Bulgaria's naval force.

DENMARK

Elephanten

Danish lystfregat

Built in 1687, in Copenhagen, by the English shipwright Francis Sheldon, then working in Denmark, for King Christian V. Length 28·2m, beam 7m, depth of hold 2·8m. Rigged as a snow, with two masts.

Denmark's history as a monarchy is, of course, interwoven with that of her Scandinavian neighbours, but her greater nearness to the Continent and French and German machinations, has meant that she has remained a small, mostly rich, and populous Scandinavian power. As a nation with a long seafaring tradition, however, her fleet was always a force to be taken seriously. During the period from about AD 850, Denmark's system of monarchy has changed through hierarchical election, and absolutism to constitutional, and at the time that the idea of the royal yacht was reaching the courts of Europe, King Christian V ruled Denmark as an absolute monarch.

King Christain V's pleasure vessel the *Elephanten*, the dockyard model of which is illustrated and said to have been made by Francis Sheldon, is in keeping with Dutch and English yachts of the period, with her steep sheer aft, and the ornate decoration skilfully lavished on her, particularly on the stern which housed the royal quarters. The resplendent elephant, complete with howdah and centred between palm trees, occupied a place of honour below a finial crown and the royal arms below. This was the insignia of a knightly 'Order of the Elephant', revived in the seventeenth century. The model is an excellent example of the good design of Danish ships of the period, and the absence of hull planking shows her very sturdy construction. Her decoration contains a rather more regulated form of sculpture and devices, and seems to have a greater seagoing quality about it compared to contemporary Dutch decoration.

Elephanten's rig as a 'snow' – which in England in the eighteenth century normally described a small brig with fore and aft mizzen, and with yards on her bowsprit – probably meant that she was in most respects similar to the English 'ketch'. In commission she carried eighteen 6-pounder guns on her main deck, and six 4-pounders on her quarter deck. In 1690, a new yacht was launched – the *Cronen*– which was bigger and more seaworthy. From 1703, *Elephanten* was used by the Danish Navy until, in 1721, she was wrecked and became a total loss.

Slesvig

Built by Robert Napier in Glasgow in 1845, as
Copenhagen. *Loa 54m, beam 7·85m, draught
2·5m (est). Hull rigged as three-masted schooner.
Displacement tonnage: 740. Engines: steam,
side-lever type (Napier) of 240 nhp, giving 10
knots. Paddle-wheels 13m in diameter.*

For Denmark, the mid-nineteenth century
was a period of continued political, social and
economic reform; the resurgence of the
Slesvig-Holstein problems; and the advance
of industrial ideas brought by the Age of
Steam in Europe. The repeal of the English
Navigation Acts in 1863, brought an upsurge
of merchant shipping, and following the
appearance of the Clyde built *Caledonia* –

plying between Copenhagen and Kiel as
early as 1819 – the number of Danish steam
ships rose to forty-three by 1862. It was in
keeping with the current trend in Europe that
Denmark's royal yachts should be steam
driven.

At first, the *Copenhagen* was used in the
packet-boat service between Kiel and Copenhagen, and then from 1848, when she was
acquired by the navy, and renamed *Slesvig*,
she had a varied career which included her
use for towing, the transportation of troops
and as a mail boat. In 1856, she was approved
by King Christian IX as a royal yacht, and
was equipped as such, and used by him until
1879, with the exception of the year 1864, in

which she was armed with twelve 3-pounder guns, and did duty as a tender to the screw frigate *Niels Juel* and the iron-clad *Dannebrog*, during the Slesvig-Holstein War.

The illustration shows *Slesvig* steaming out of Kieler Fjord, with a view of the Castle and Nicolai Church to the left, and the brig, under way on the right, is a reminder that sail had not yet conceded the victory of steam. This modest steam yacht typifies the paddle-wheeler of the period, developing from early Clydeside conceptions, for the engines of which Robert Napier did so much, by his ingenious modifications of the primitive beam engine.

In many respects *Slesvig* is similar to Britain's first royal steam yacht, the *Victoria and Albert I*, and in her, many delightful hours must have been spent by Denmark's king and royal family, in that gem of all cruising waters – the Baltic. By 1879, she was withdrawn as a royal yacht, and finally broken up in 1894.

Built in Copenhagen by Burmeister & Wain in 1879, for King Christian IX. Loa 199ft, beam 26·8ft, depth 10·4ft, Steel hull, rigged with two masts. TM Tonnage: 658. Engines: compound steam, four cylinders, giving 376 nhp; built by Burmeister & Wain.

By the 1880s, the paddle-steamer had reached an apogee of design and function which remained static to the present day, when, alas, these handsome and popular vessels have all but completely disappeared from Europe's coastal waters.

In the *Dannebrog*, Denmark had a royal yacht of modest size, but in keeping with those of other monarchies of the period, particularly Britain, Germany and Austria. With her raked funnels and masts, and her general design, in many respects she had a greater elegance and yacht-like appearance than her royal contemporaries. This may be seen in the context of the steady economic growth in Denmark up to 1914, of which one of the most important aspects was shipbuilding. The heart of this was the traditional engineering foundation of Burmeister & Wain, which also built a later *Dannebrog* and the huge steam yacht *Standart* for Imperial Russia, and among an increasing steam merchant fleet, the world's first motor ship.

Yachting had been well established in Denmark by the founding, in 1866, of the Kongelig Dansk (Royal Danish) yacht club under royal patronage, and during his reign, King Christian IX was also a member of the British Royal Yacht Squadron. He often appeared at Cowes Week in *Dannebrog*, which, during the years when there was a change to bigger screw-driven royal yachts, took on an old-fashioned look – as did *Victoria and Albert II* – on these occasions of regal display. Julius Gabe, in *Yachting* written in 1902, reflects this general attitude: 'the King of Denmark's *Dannebrog*, a schooner rigged paddle-boat, is by no means a regal craft.' Despite this however, the yacht continued to serve successive Danish monarchs until, in

1931, she was replaced by a more modern screw motor yacht.

The name *Dannebrog* is that of a Danish order of chivalrous knighthood, which, like the 'Order of the Elephant', was revived in seventeenth-century Denmark. It appears in use for two royal yachts and the armour-clad frigate of that name in the Danish Navy of the 1860s.

Dannebrog
twin-screw schooner

Built in 1931 by the Royal Dockyard Copenhagen, for King Christian X. Loa 207·2ft, beam 34·1ft, draught 11·8ft. Steel hull rigged with two masts. TM Tonnage: 1070. Engines: two 4-cylinder diesels, built by Burmeister & Wain.

The second *Dannebrog* is a fine example of yacht design which reached a peak in the early 1900s, making a final appearance in about 1930. The steam screw schooner was noted for its retention of the clipper-ship hull shape, with its raked and flared bow, long, flowing unbroken sheerline ending aft in a long overhang counter. To this was added a funnel which had to be of just the right height and size, and with a rake conforming with that of the masts. With deckhouse profiles kept low and following the hull sheer, and with the finishing touch of a slightly steeved up bowsprit, there is nothing that has since had the same elegant grace and panache as this style of power yacht.

Dannebrog will be seen to qualify in all these respects, with the exception that she has a broken sheer line, which although not detracting from her good looks, when combined with her diesel engine propulsion, puts her into the motor yacht class. In all respects she is a fine royal yacht, and a tribute to Danish building. Surviving the disasters of World War II, since 1947 she was used by the late Danish monarch – King Frederick IX – for state visits and family cruising, generally in the Baltic. In July 1957, *Dannebrog* was seen and admired by thousands of Londoners as she lay in the Pool of London, waiting to take home for the summer holidays a Danish princess who was then attending an English boarding school, and she was also recently seen at Greenwich, bringing Queen Margrethe on her State visit.

Denmark today is a very democratic constitutional monarchy. There are no great displays of regal pomp, and the royal yacht is looked upon as a symbol of the part which the monarch and his family plays in the life of the country. As elsewhere in Europe, popular yachting, particularly small boat racing has developed enormously, and the Danish royal family take an enthusiastic and informal part in it. There have been many small yachts built for royalty, like the 17 ton Bermudian sloop *Rita V*, by the well known Scandinavian firm of Anker & Jensen in 1930 for King Christian X.

In 1897, Dixon Kemp, commenting on the sport of yachting in Denmark, notes its strong development, and the excellence of the yachts. It is not surprising that this should be so when an ancient seafaring tradition and the Baltic are Denmark's heritage.

EGYPT

Mahroussa
and
Kassed Kheir

screw schooner;

paddle-yacht

Built by Samuda Bros., London, in 1865. Loa 478 ft (in 1905), beam 42.6ft, draught 17.5 ft. Iron hull. TM tonnage: 3658 (1905).

"MAHROU

Designed and built by Thornycrofts' at Southampton in 1926. Loa 237.7 ft, beam 32 ft, draught 3.5 ft. Steel hull. TM tonnage: 1,111.

"KASSE

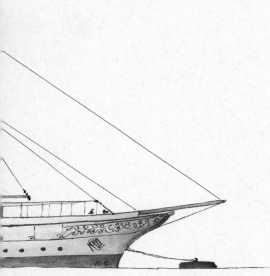

Engines: Oscillating steam paddle (1865). Three Parsons Steam Turbines (1905) – 6,500 bhp.

EIR"

Engines: triple-expansion steam driving paddle-wheels.

For technical details see illustration. The text for Kassed Kheir *is on p38.*

When Mohammed Ali defeated the Mamelukes who had ruled Egypt under Turkish suzerainty, he created a dynasty which gave the country a succession of monarchs who ruled, generally with little thought but for self-aggrandisement, for 148 years – the last seventy-eight with help and protection from a not over-eager, but involved, Britain. Whatever their political shortcomings, Egypt's kings were colourful despots, spending lavishly on personal pleasure. They were quick to see the assets that steam yachts could have in their luxurious, though often somewhat insecure, tenure of Egypt's throne.

Paddle-yacht *Mahroussa* was acquired in 1865, and subsequently was given two complete face-lifts; once in 1906, when she was lengthened to 420ft, given triple-screw steam turbine propulsion, and an increased displacement of 3,417 tons (appearing then as in the illustration). About 1950, her upper works and funnel were given a modern look this time in Italy – the earlier work was done in Glasgow. Still in use by the Egyptian Republic, as a training ship, *Mahroussa* can boast of being not only the oldest steam yacht still in commission, but also one of the largest ever built.

King Farouk, 1936–52, became a regal anachronism and thus the target of the world's Press. Royal yacht *Mahroussa* became for the 'last of the pharoahs' the only moderately safe means of escaping publicity. Throughout his reign the old yacht served him well, and there were many romantic cruises concealing amorous assignments of the sort with which his name was continually connected. In latter years when there was good reason for him to suppose that a coup d'état might mean his violent end, *Mahroussa* was kept, like a gangster's get-away-car, with steam up and moorings shortened; but on the one occasion on which he might have used her thus, he found that the yacht's batteries had been taken ashore for charging!

When in 1952, King Farouk, his queen and family steamed off into exile, it was virtually the last time *Mahroussa* would serve a king. If yachts were capable of soliloquy, she might have remembered better times when, with the accompanying royal yachts of several of the great monarchs of nineteenth-century Europe, she had carried King Ismail as host through the newly opened Suez Canal.

Safa-El-Bahr   screw schooner

Built in 1894 by Messrs A & J Inglis of Glasgow, for Khedive Abbas II. Loa 221ft, beam 27·1ft, draught 12ft. Steel hull rigged with two masts. TM tonnage: 669. Engines: triple-expansion steam, fed by two Scotch boilers, giving 1200 ihp, and a speed of 14·1 knots.

This handsome screw yacht, luxuriously fitted out on two decks, joined *Mahroussa* as an Egyptian royal yacht in 1894 when the latter was already in her twenty-ninth year of service. She appears to have been used for rather more informal occasions, and while the older yacht was in Glasgow for alterations. There is no doubt that any Egyptian monarch must have delighted in the proximity of his country to so many delectable cruising areas. With all the Mediterranean seas on his doorstep of Alexandria, it was to the Sea of Marmara to which Abbas II constantly directed *Safa-El-Bahr*. His pro-Turkish attitudes however, caused his deposition from the throne of Egypt when in World War I Turkey joined the central powers, and he remained in that country.

That father of the British package tour – Thomas Cook – whose paddle-steamers on the Nile appear briefly in history at the relief of Khartoum, seems to have set a standard of interior decoration in yachts which was

followed slavishly in detail by successive Egyptian monarchs. When the paddle-yacht *Kassed Kheir* (see pp36-7 for illustration) was ordered from Messrs Thornycrofts (now Vosper Thornycroft) of Southampton, strict instructions were given that the interior decoration and fittings should be of the traditional 'Victorian regal splendour' as supplied by Messrs Waring & Gillow of London, and that the design of the yacht should be as near as possible to those used by Thomas Cook on the Nile.

In 1926, the *Kassed Kheir*, being of shallow draught, was built in sections and shipped out as deck cargo to be reassembled and launched on the Nile. With her conservative looks, which somehow seemed right for her surroundings, the new Egyptian royal yacht saw much service on the river. In her, King Fuad, and later his son Farouk, made elaborately arranged and escorted tours of the Upper Nile.

Of all European royal yachts, *Kassed Kheir* was perhaps the most specialised, but she still had all the outward show of her contemporaries – decorative gingerbread at bow and stern, and the elaborate display of the royal arms on her paddle-boxes. She ended her days as an annex to a Cairo hotel in 1958.

FRANCE

The Versailles Flotilla

A contemporary print showing the vessels which comprised the 'Flotille sur le Grand Canal'.

During the years 1643 to 1715, King Louis XIV – 'Le Roi Soleil' – created for France the role of the mother of European culture in the spirit of the earlier Renaissance in Italy, but in this case Louis XIV was firmly the dictator of the arts. The great palace at Versailles, which set a fashion for most of royal Europe, remains a memorial to this age in France. Less well known perhaps is that part of the vast grounds of the palace 'Le Grand Canal', formed from about 1669 as a great expanse of water some 1,560m long and 120m wide, surrounded by formal gardens, subtly wrought pavilions with flights of steps

leading to the water; walks, vantage points, and fountains.

To provide a flotilla of small vessels for the pleasure and entertainment of the king and his court, an army of tradesmen were employed to build *chaloupes et galiotes* (launches and barges), and their decoration was the charge of leading painters, sculptors and gilders. In 1679, a number of highly ornate *gondoles* arrived from Venice to swell the flotilla – complete with colourfully dressed gondoliers. At this time also there is mention of *yaks* making an appearance, and small 'frigates' of a size which enabled them to be manned and manoeuvred on the Canal.

The *yaks* were in fact English yachts of the period, and built at Deptford. One of them was a personal gift from Charles II to the French king (the English monarch had forgotten to pay for it – by an oversight it is hoped), and it is likely that at this time they would have been of 'ketch' rig. There was no doubt about their seaworthiness as they were sailed to Le Havre, and thence transported overland to Versailles. These yachts caused great interest in France, although yachting had developed beyond a pattern started in Holland earlier in the century.

The yachts, the small 'frigates', the oar-propelled *chaloupes*, the *galiotes* and *gondoles* assembled on the Grand Canal at Versailles, were used to provide a marine spectacle – a sort of nautical *concours d'élégance*; and an occasion for the royal inspection of manoeuvres and mock sea-battles. Enormous sums of money were poured into the creation of the flotilla. Splendid and costly materials of all kinds, and fabrics embroidered in gold and silver, were drawn from all over Europe to create for King Louis XIV and his courtiers a spectacle in keeping with the fabulous conceptions of the Versailles Palace.

Le Canot Imperial

Built from designs by Guillemare, in 1811. Loa 17·21m, beam 3·35m, draught 0·97m. Propelled by twenty-six oarsmen. Wooden construction.

Up to the Revolution of 1789 there were no official French royal yachts, and although in the creation of the First Empire there was a powerful French Navy, Napoleon Bonaparte

was completely absorbed with his activities as the supreme general of his armies. His one concession to appearing in something akin to a yacht was the order given in 1811 for the construction of *Le Canot Impérial* for the purpose of an imperial inspection of the defences of the port of Antwerp.

The hull of the vessel was built in the incredibly short time of three weeks, and then the ornamentation was applied and the saloon fitted aft. The whole effect of *Le Canot* is elegant and impressive. From the group of allegorical figures at the prow – Neptune astride a sea-beast, attended by cherubs – the sheer runs smoothly aft to the imperial arms elaborately conceived. The saloon, classically simple, is surmounted by a great imperial crown supported by cherubs. It will be noticed that the blades of the oars are decorated, and that those of the starboard oarsmen carry a different device from those of the port side.

As mentioned earlier, a vessel propelled by oars cannot really be classed as a yacht, but *Le Canot Impérial* does represent a particular kind of royal barge which, in the past, and even today, has a place among royal accoutrements. The royal barge of France has survived the years and two World Wars, and despite the difficulties existing in 1943, *Le Canot* was brought by rail to Paris. In order to get her into the Musée Marine at the Palais de Chaillot, a wall had to be knocked down.

The illustration shows the original *Canot Impérial* as she now appears in the Musée Marine. Full sized wax figures of her crew and passengers have been skilfully made and placed to show a re-enactment of a state visit to the port of Brest in August 1858. On this occasion, the royal passengers are Emperor Napoleon III (Bonaparte's nephew) and his Empress Eugénie, who can be seen standing holding a parasol just forward of the saloon doors.

It is perhaps fitting that the last royal couple of France, Napoleon III and his empress, should perpetuate a memory of *Le Canot*, because during their reign France saw, really for the first time, the use of royal yachts.

L'Aigle   paddle-schooner

Built in 1858 in France. Loa 160ft (est), beam 25ft (est), draught 10ft (est). Hull rigged as a three-masted schooner. Engines: simple, oscillating, steam, driving paddle-wheels.

In 1852, Prince Louis Napoleon, the master of the coup d'état, proclaimed himself Emperor Napoleon III, and the Second Empire began in France. From that date until his abdication at the end of the Franco-Prussian War, this enigmatic personality who seems to have somewhat baffled his contemporary sovereigns and historians alike, above all believed in and worked continuously to achieve the greatness of France as a world power.

During the Second Empire French industry was developed and the new steam technology put to valuable use in railways and ships. Particularly in the latter field of shipbuilding France moved ahead, and her navy benefitted from innovations and new techniques. It was in keeping with these moves that the *Aigle*, French built, should have made her appearance as the first imperial yacht.

Paddle-schooner *L'Aigle* was a reliable and comfortable vessel. With her black hull relieved with gilding at her eagle figure-head, the moulded strakes which ran the length of her hull and the white of the insides of the row of imitation gunports – really shuttered portholes – she is much in keeping with the style of royal paddle-yachts of the period. The emperor made many cruises in her, including a visit

to Venice, which gave him a chance to re-
cuperate from the burdens of state which
continually stretched his physical and mental
resources.

On the 16 November 1869, the first royal
yacht of France was most fittingly present at
an event which marked an achievement, by
the great French engineer Ferdinand de
Lesseps, of immense future international
importance – the opening of the newly com-
pleted Suez Canal. The emperor was said to
be too busy to attend, and so it was the
Empress Eugénie (appropriately de Lesseps

was her cousin) who represented Imperial
France.

At 8am, on the morning of 18 November,
the Canal was declared open, and *L'Aigle*,
carrying the empress, led the ceremonial fleet
of ships slowly through the Desert of Ismailia.
In that fleet were the royal yachts of King
Ismail of Egypt, and of the Austrian Emperor
Franz Joseph – paddle-yachts *Mahroussa* and
Fantasie, as well as a large number of smaller
steam yachts and screw-frigates of represented
navies.

Built in France, possibly at Le Havre in 1859 originally as Cassard. *Loa 230ft (est), beam 24ft (est), draught 12ft (est). Iron hull rigged as a barquentine. Engines: estimated simple steam or early two stage expansion, fed by French fire-tube boilers, and driving a single screw of large diameter.*

This yacht which bore the name of Napoleon III's cousin – Prince Jérôme Napoléon – was an example of the type of steam ship that began to appear in Europe and America about this time. The superior propulsion power of the screw over paddle-wheels did not immediately banish sail, and the very substantial quality of masts, spars and sails of this yacht – and the other shipping seen in the background of the illustration – shows clearly that steam power at sea was still only a very useful auxiliary.

Used concurrently with the older *Aigle*, and with the increasingly important role of France in the Mediterranean, *Jérôme Napoléon* may well have been in demand by members of the imperial family. It is likely that, as in other yachts of this period, her accommodation was on one deck, with the deck house, seen aft, used as a day-saloon.

It is tempting to speculate whether it was this yacht which, carrying her namesake, Prince Jérôme, arrived in Turin in 1859. The occasion was his wedding to the fifteen year old Princess Glotilde – daughter of King Victor Emmanuel of Piedmont and Sardinia – an arrangement seen by historians as a human sacrifice made by the king, in his efforts to gain French assistance for his continuous efforts to unite Italy. At all events the married couple seem to have departed by sea for what could have been a honeymoon cruise in the yacht.

The growing importance to France of Mediterranean North Africa, particularly Algeria, and the knowledge that the emperor made visits there, make it likely that he used *Jérôme Napoléon* for them. During some periods it is possible that this vessel was used as a despatch ship by the growing French Navy.

On all counts, screw barquentine *Jérôme Napoléon* does not give the impression of being more than a naval auxiliary in use as a royal yacht. She lacks the good looks and panache of the steam yacht, and in 1867 a vessel was acquired and used as the imperial yacht, which had much more of these desirable qualities.

La Reine Hortense

Built in Le Havre, by the firm of Normand, originally as Patriote. *Similar to* Jérôme Napoléon *in size and engine power, but most likely of wooden construction.*

It is difficult to state the exact date when this yacht was built. Originally *Patriote*, then *Comte d'Eu*, and *Cassard*, she appears as the imperial yacht *La Reine Hortense* in 1867. She looks older than the *Jérôme Napoléon*, but is in all respects a more elegant yacht, with the elaborate imperial pavilion in the 'Empire' style built on her upper deck abaft the main-mast. She is much in the early traditions of the sail and steam period, previously mentioned. The scene depicted in the illustration, with the presence of the ship-of-the-line *L'Austerlitz* under way on the right, underlines a period in French naval history.

During the Second Empire, growing French naval power was a disturbing factor among her contemporary powers in Europe – including Britain. Her screw ships-of-war had superior engine power and speed, and during the Crimean War, her ships – particularly the battleship *Charlemagne* – were the only vessels

which could steam through the Bosphorus irrespective of the set of the notorious current through those straits or the strength of the wind – a feat of which the British Fleet was at that time incapable.

Napoleon III was a member of the Royal Yacht Squadron, and it is not unlikely that he and his empress appeared in the *Reine Hortense* at some Cowes Weeks. Certainly the empress was keen on steam yachts, since after exile she owned the *Thistle* and was often seen at Cowes and the Riviera in the years before 1914. Her rescue from France after the debacle of Sedan, was in most part due to a member of the Royal Yacht Squadron, Sir John Burgoyne who, with his wife, were storm-bound in Deauville awaiting a chance to sail for England, in the old cutter *Gazelle*.

Late on the night of 2 September 1870, with all the trappings of a cloak and dagger episode, Sir John found himself with the fugitive Empress Eugénie aboard committed to sail that night. In spite of gale force winds, *Gazelle* and her crew were up to the emergency, and Empress Eugénie reached Cowes next day, and there began for her and the emperor the exile during which she was left a widow. In her later yachting days in the steam yacht *Thistle* she often had occasion to say to her captain: 'When I last landed here I was an empress.' *La Reine Hortense* was the last royal yacht of France.

GERMANY

Kaiseradler

paddle-schooner

Built in Germany at Kiel by 'Germania' in 1875. Loa 268ft, beam 34ft, draught 14ft. Iron hull rigged with two masts. Engines: oscillating 2-cylinder steam, working paddle-wheels; 3,000 ihp, fire-tube boilers; speed 15 knots (est).

When Wilhelm II succeeded to the throne of the young German Empire which had been declared in 1871, the road which Germany took from his enthronement in 1888, has been much discussed and analysed by historians – generally with adverse conclusions. What is not denied, however, is the Kaiser's part in the creation of Germany's sea power, and the personal part which he played in encouraging his nation to share his enthusiasm for yachting. This latter activity has borne fruit in the prominent part which Germans play in international yachting today.

The paddle-yacht *Kaiseradler* was provided in 1875, at a time when the second, and final, period of the paddle-steamer was in vogue for royal yachts in Europe. She shows much of the features of the times, particularly the shuttered gunport portholes, and she was substantially built and fitted out with accommodation and decoration in the Prussian *altdeutsch* – strictly masculine style, then in vogue. The curious bell-mouthed funnel tops are unmistakably Teutonic and were repeated in the later *Hohenzollern* (see p50).

Germany's yachting antecendents were somewhat slim. In 1855 the Segel Club 'Rhe' had

been formed, but sailing was mostly restricted to Alster Lake. The Norddeutscher Regatta Verein, of which Empress Frederick was royal patron, was founded in 1868, and some activity undertaken in Baltic regattas. At such functions, in the *Kaiseradler* or the small screw yacht *Grille*, Kaiser Wilhelm II took some part in the early days of his reign.

As Queen Victoria's grandson, and with the Prince of Wales his uncle, the Kaiser almost automatically became a member of the British Royal Yacht Squadron, and it was from his experiences at Cowes Week that he began to assume his role as a keen yachtsman, and his dream of outshining the rest of Europe – and in particular Britain – in all aspects of royal yachting.

The Kaiser, with plans for a great German Navy, saw to it that the great Vulcan ship-building concern, which had been allowed to run down, was revived. Later this yard was to build for him the big steam yacht – the impressive *Hohenzollern*.

Grille

screw schooner

Built in Germany in the 1880s (est). Loa 160ft (est), beam 19·5ft (est), draught 9ft (est). Wooden hull rigged with three masts. Engines (est) : two compound steam, driving twin screws.

The growth of yachting in Germany, and the emperor's keenness to establish a marine tradition meant that there were a number of vessels, either built as yachts, or which served as such, generally in use at the same time as their more spectacular sisters were holding the limelight. *Grille* is one such yacht, and unfortunately, very little appears to be known about her, not being listed in Lloyds for the period when she was certainly in commission.

It seems most likely that *Grille* was used for the occasions when Kaiser Wilhelm II visited his growing fleet in the Baltic – the canvas-shrouded pavilion seen aft suggests this. The general shape of *Grille* gives the impression more of a small warship rather than a yacht. She looks fast, and the tumblehome of her hull gives her something of the panache of a gunboat.

Serving at the same time as *Grille* was the *Alexandria,* a twin screw yacht of 99 TM tons and loa of 91·9ft. The fact that she was built at Stettin, by the firm of Aron & Gollnow in 1887, with a steel hull, underlines the preliminaries which were later to appear in the Imperial German High Seas Fleet. German yacht building made a somewhat late start compared to British, and in the first Kiel Regattas under the emperor's patronage, yachts owned for racing were ex-British or American. William II's empress owned the steel-hulled schooner *Iduna,* which had been *Yampa,* built in Wilmington USA by Harlan & Hollingsworth to designs of A. Cary Smith in 1887. But there were gradual improvements made both in yacht building and also in the training of yacht hands and skippers who were finally to take over all the Kaiser's yachts. A most interesting German innovation was the making of the 14-ton auxiliary screw yawl *Alumina.* This yacht, built for Prince Wilhelm zu Wied, was completely revolutionary at the time (1895) since she was made entirely of aluminium, a material which appears to have many desirable qualities for yacht construction.

It seems strange that the German nation did not produce a competitive yacht building industry. Perhaps their true genius lay in building warships. Certainly all the steam yachts which were built for the Kaiser have that particular flavour.

Built by the Vulcan Shipbuilding Company, in Stettin in 1893, to German Admiralty designs. Loa 382·6ft, beam 45·9ft, draught 23·1ft. Steel hull rigged with three masts. TM tonnage: 3,773. Engines: two triple-expansion steam, giving 9,500 ihp, and a speed of 21·5 knots, fed by eight Scotch boilers; engines by Vulcan-Stettin.

By 1895, the German emperor could boast the biggest and most powerful royal steam yacht in Europe, and in the newly opened Kiel Canal, a quick route for his navy from the Baltic to the North Sea. The huge sums involved in the building of the new yacht caused objections in the Reichstag, and were only finally approved when it was agreed that the *Hohenzollern* should, if the occasion arose, be available to the navy as a despatch vessel! The time had now come when the Kaiser could arrive at Cowes in a style which he thought put him well above his regal peers in temporal pomp and imperial prestige.

The illustration of *Hohenzollern* is an impressive, and not often seen view of this huge yacht. As she turns sharply to starboard, the activity on board, coupled with the sight of her boats swung out and boat-boom rigged, suggests that she is just arriving at Cowes. Her whole appearance is one of a warship and not a yacht. Bell-mouthed funnel tops are an echo of *Kaiseradler,* and with her 'ram' bow with its imperial double-eagle crest and gilded decoration – which seems out of place in such a vessel – turtle-back forecastle and her general look of aggressive sturdiness, she is unmistakably German. But it cannot be denied that she was very impressive.

Hohenzollern did a lot of sea-time from the Mediterranean to the Baltic and North Seas. In 1902, Prince Henry of Prussia – a keen and very able yachtsman – arrived in her in the USA, for the launching of the Kaiser's first racing schooner, *Meteor III* – designed by the American, Cary Smith. There were often occasions when the steam yachts of other sovereigns were anchored near the Kaiser's *Hohenzollern,* and by 1913, both the Russian *Standart* and Britain's *Victoria and Albert III* were bigger.

The German emperor's reaction of course was to jump ahead once more, and it is a fact that a new steam yacht, of a projected length of 520ft, and a displacement tonnage of 7,300, was in fact laid down in the Vulcan-Stettin yards. She was, by all accounts, to have been a superb vessel much more in the true steam yacht style, with clipper bow and counter stern. World War I prevented further work being done on her, and in a state which precluded her sale, she was broken up in 1923.

Built in Germany at Kiel in 1909, by Germania Werst, to designs by Max Oertz. Loa 129·2ft, beam 27·15ft, draught 14·8ft. Steel hull rigged as a two-masted, gaff topsail schooner. Sails made by Mahlitz. TM tonnage : 400.

Kaiser Wilhelm II, for all his bombast and self-assertion, which did not endear him to his contemporaries, was a genuinely keen and able racing yachtsman. His peculiar 'love-hate' reactions to all things British, and particularly his obvious admiration for the atmosphere of Cowes Regatta Week, at which, a tough, yet gentlemanly sporting activity was coupled with an indefinable noblesse oblige, led to the founding of the Imperial Yacht Club, and Kiel Regatta Week, under his patronage.

Kiel Week became fashionable but lacked the traditional qualities of Cowes, as so many implanted functions do. Within the space of some ten years, the Kaiser had owned five big yachts – all named, or renamed *Meteor* – from the first cutter (ex *Thistle*), to the final *Meteor V*, a schooner similar to the illustration. His over-riding desire was to win races and outdo 'Uncle Bertie' (King Edward VII), and it was his domineering rudeness at Cowes Regattas, together with new, and controversial yacht club rules, which caused the Prince of Wales (as he then was) to give up racing and sell *Britannia* in 1897.

The illustration of the German built and manned *Meteor IV* speaks for itself – a breath-taking sight to thrill even the most confirmed landlubber. She epitomises a period, in the years prior to 1914, when the appearance of such yachts sharply divided opinion as to the kind of racing rules which could be applied in handicapping and rating without narrowing the sporting qualities of yacht racing.

It has been said that Kaiser Wilhelm II did much to establish a German yachting tradition, and this is borne out by the sight of *Meteor IV*. Gradually from the days of the first cutter with an all British crew and skipper, German yacht hands had been trained to take over. In 1929, looking back to earlier days, that sagacious and experienced yachtsman, B. Heckstall-Smith could concede that the German skippers and crews of *Meteor*s IV and *V* were up to the highest standards of contemporary British and Scandinavian yachts-men. 1918 saw the end of Imperial Germany, and the Kaiser exiled in Holland, but the tradition of yachting was rooted and continues to grow.

GREECE

Dragon Class Yacht

International One Design

Loa 8·9m, beam 1·96m, draught 1·2m. Mast height 10·5m, sail area 23·2sq m. Original designer the late Johann Anker.

The illustration of a Dragon class yacht – one of hundreds of this popular design – would remind Greeks of an event in the Olympic Games sail racing held in Naples Bay in the summer of 1960 in which Crown Prince Constantine of Greece succeeded in beating his Italian rival to win a gold medal. He was sailing the Dragon class yacht which had been presented to him by the Royal Greek Navy, in which he trained himself to the high standard necessary to compete in an important event like the Olympic sailing races.

Greece finally won her freedom from Turkish dominance in 1828, and from that time she became a kingdom. But the national character of her people has shown a tendency to be undecided whether in fact a monarchy was the best kind of solution to her political problems. With an imported royal house, with King Ortho as the first Greek monarch, there have been many occasions when Greek royal families have been ousted – sometimes temporarily – in favour of political strong-men like Venizelos, Metaxas, and then the colonels.

When Prince Constantine won the Olympic Gold Medal for Greece, there was naturally great celebration and Queen Frederika has recorded in her memoirs that she and King Paul were overjoyed that their son had achieved such a distinction for his nation. This aspect of informal royal yachting is further borne out by the keenness for sailing small boats which was shared by King Paul and his family. Unfortunately there is little information about the part that formal royal yachts have played in Greece.

King George II, who was deposed by the republic in 1924, and came back to rule in 1933, seems likely to have used an elderly steam yacht named *Sfakteria* for formal occasions. He was certainly a member of the British Royal Yacht Squadron, and appeared at Cowes Week in this yacht, although contemporary opinion thought her rather unregal. Paul, who succeeded his brother George in 1947, was very much a sailor, and delighted in small boat handling – in particular his fast modern 'crash boat'. His son Constantine showed in no uncertain terms that he had inherited the same innate yachting ability.

ITALY

Savoia I screw barquentine

*Built at Castellammare di Stabia, in June 1883.
Loa 304·9ft, beam 41·4ft. Hull rigged with
three masts as a barquentine. Displacement
tonnage: 3,266. Engines: built by Penn of
London, steam, 3-cylinder horizontal, fed by
eight boilers giving 3,340 hp, and a speed of
15·2 knots.*

Italy's history as a united nation begins in
1862 with King Victor Emmanuel II achieving
his goal at last, with the tyrannical Austrians
expelled and the Papal State of Rome liberated
from a corrupt and politically repressive
Papal Court. In the years that followed, Italy,
as a monarchy, took her place in the royal
circles of Europe, and moved into an era
of industrial development, particularly in the
north.

Official royal yachts were soon forthcoming,
and two of them were called *Savoia* – from
the royal house of Savoy of the Italian

monarchs. King Umberto I seems to have
been the first recipient of the symbol which
Italy's status now demanded, and the yacht
was the screw barquentine *Savoia I*. She
was built in the ancient harbour of Castell-
lammare di Stabia, redolent with memories
of the last days of Pompeii, and Roman
shipbuilding. An imposing vessel of size and
character, she looks more like a sailing
merchantman than a steam yacht of the
period, but she has a dignity which befitted
her function.

With Italy's magnificent seaboard, *Savoia*
was much used for state occasions and visits
in the Mediterranean and Adriatic seas. She
seems to have served her purpose well, and
was a comfortable and well fitted royal yacht.
It can be seen from the illustration that she
has the same kind of shuttered square portholes which are so noticeable in the bigger

royal yachts of the period. The interior furnishing and decoration would likely have been the rather ornate style popular in Italian villas.

Savoia's ship's company consisted of ten officers and 235 petty officers and men, a reminder that all Italian official royal yachts were primarily voted from naval funds, and were part of the fleet. This procedure, of course, was followed in other European monarchies, and with certain variations there could be two kinds of royal yacht, the privately owned and the official naval unit. *Savoia* was in royal use until 1902 when she was withdrawn and, with an extensive refit and modification she became the floating workshop *Vulcan*. She was finally removed from the naval establishment in March 1923.

Trinacria
ex-merchant ship *America*

Built on the Clyde by the firm of J & G Thomson Ltd in 1883, originally for the British merchant service. Loa 462·8ft, beam 50·7ft. Mild steel hull (est) rigged with two masts. Displacement tonnage: 9,199. Engines: 3-cylinder double expansion steam, fed by six boilers, producing 6,120 hp, and giving 15 knots. Engines also built by Thomson's.

Acquired by the Italian Navy in 1887, the British merchant ship *America* was renamed *Trinacria* by a ministerial order of 29 November 1891, and after a very comprehensive refit, she replaced *Savoia I* as the official Italian royal yacht in 1900.

By any standards *Trinacria* was an impressive

vessel to be used as a yacht. During her refit, she appears to have been given some of the traditional features which distinguish yachts from their merchant sisters. Her shelter deck may have been extended, and she was given a figure-head and its attendant gingerbread decoration, and a bowsprit to go with her clipper bow. It is likely that her hull was constructed from mild steel, since her builders had used that metal in the Cunard liner *Servia* – which vessel won the Atlantic Blue Riband in her day. The turtle-deck forecastle and the after steering shelter were also features of ships built at that time by J & G Thomson Ltd.

The size of *Trinacria,* and her ship's company of eighteen officers, 371 petty officers and men, together with the fact that she carried four 57mm, and four (later reduced to two) 37mm guns, suggests that the Italian Navy were slightly more concerned with her possible use as an armed cruiser in the event of war, than with her role as a royal yacht. But as the latter she was used in Italian waters and may well have appeared further afield in the first decades of the twentieth century.

In 1925, by an order of 16 July, *Trinacria* was withdrawn from service completely, having by that time become old fashioned in design and difficult and expensive to maintain to high standards. The vessel which replaced her as the Italian royal yacht was in every respect worthy of that title, although by that time Mussolini and his Blackshirts had taken control of Italy and the king remained only as a puppet figure-head.

Savoia II   twin-screw schooner

Built by the Royal Italian Arsenal, Spezia in 1922, as the Cita di Palermo. *Loa 390ft, beam 49·2ft, draught 15ft (est). Steel hull rigged with two masts. TM tonnage: 4,388. Engines: one Parson's steam turbine geared to two shafts, fed by eight Yarrow boilers, giving 12,000 hp and a speed of 22 knots.*

At Palermo in 1925, *Cita di Palermo* was converted to a royal yacht by Cantieri Navali Riuniti, and renamed *Savoia* to be put into service for King Victor Emmanuel III. Perhaps significantly the classification as 'royal yacht' was changed to 'royal warship' in 1926, and she then carried four 76/40mm guns. But this did not change her role as transport for the king on many occasions when she was used for official functions. It appears that she was also used for a while, as a floating exhibition of the wonders of Italy's fascist regime.

Savoia II was a magnificent steam yacht, and the illustration shows that she was in the best traditions of that class of vessel. With accommodation on three decks, fitted out *par excellence,* there were few other European royal yachts that were her equal for size or elegance. She had many innovations in styling which reflected the increasing skill of Italian naval architects, a factor which has certainly grown in the world of yacht design, particularly so in recent years, and in the realm of a new breed of motor yacht.

Following the general trend in the monarchies of Europe in the nineteenth century, the Regio Yacht Club Italiano was established in 1879 in the early days of the reign of King Umberto I; but it was Victor Emmanual III, who succeeded him in 1900, who was the enthusiastic patron of yachting. In the years before and after World War I, when yachting became fashionably popular in Italy, the king privately owned two steam yachts consecutively, both called *Iela.* The renowned Commandatore Marconi owned a 500 tonner, and the Duke of Abruzzi was also a well known and keen yachtsman, whose name appears as Vice-Commodore of the Regio Yacht Club when his monarch was its commodore.

Savoia II served in World War II as a gunboat, and her subsequent activities are not known, but at the liberation of Italy, with the king soon to abdicate in favour of the present republic, his most splendid royal yacht was found lying at the bottom of the Adriatic Sea. She had been sunk by Allied bombs off Ancona, and was struck off a reduced Italian navy list in 1947.

MONACO

Princesse Alice

Designed and built by R & H Green Ltd London, in 1891. Loa 180ft, beam 27ft, draught 12ft (est). Composite hull with steel frames, rigged as a three-masted topsail schooner. TM tonnage: 593. Engines: simple expansion 3-cylinder steam, built by J. Penn & Sons Ltd London; 64 hp, driving a single screw.

Princesse Alice seen in the illustration refitting at Cowes, replaced the 200 ton schooner *Hirondelle* for her owner, HSH Prince Albert of Monaco in 1891, and in her and a later bigger and more powerful yacht of the same name, he continued his researches into oceanography and marine biology, the sciences with which his name is internationally known and remembered. In his yachts he ranged the seas from the Equator to the Arctic Circle.

Prince Albert Honore Charles succeeded his father Prince Charles III as sovereign of the small Principality of Monaco in 1889. In his youth he had served as a lieutenant in the Spanish Navy, and during the thirty-three years of his reign he added his name to a small, but eminent number of men who have used their fine seagoing yachts to advance the frontiers of marine science. The Museum of Oceanography at Monaco is an international memorial to a royal yachtsman who was a sailor-scientist of recognised importance in this field.

It can be readily seen that *Princesse Alice* was primarily a tough seagoing sailing vessel, but this does not detract from her elegant appearance. The 'stove-pipe' funnel just before the mizzen mast, is the only indication of the steam engines which were used purely as auxiliary power. The sight of this yacht does not somehow tally with the image of Monaco's port of Monte Carlo with its fleets of expensive prestige yachts at what has become the international millionaires' club. Royal yachts for Monaco, in this context, would have no real meaning, and this has been accepted by her rulers.

Today, although it seems there is no formal royal yacht, HSH Prince Rainier, Princess Grace and their children enjoy yachting. Since he came to the throne in 1959, the prince has owned seven sizeable craft, from the 133ft *Deo Juvante* to the latest 80 ton motor yacht *Stalca*. The naming of each has become a distinct family matter, as in the case of the *Stalca*, the first two letters of which are taken from the names of the prince's children, and this scheme is repeated in most of what must be seen now as the informal royal yachts of Monaco.

THE NETHERLANDS

The Dutch Jaght

Of the seven provinces which formed the Dutch Republic freed from Spanish domination, Holland was supreme among them, and also in Europe generally, as a thrusting and opulent example of city life and commercial power. With her ports of Amsterdam and Rotterdam, strong merchant and naval fleets, and East Indies trade, she reached a peak of great influence in Europe in the seventeenth century. It was in this atmosphere of material affluence that her wealthy merchant burghers soon discovered a pastime on the natural inland waters of their native land, which took account of their need to show their prestige.

The Dutch Navy had used a type of vessel a *jachtschip* as a fast, comfortable little ship for the conveyance of despatches and of important personages. The design became modified and adapted for private use, and by the second half of the seventeenth century, the wealthy merchants' *jaghts* were of the kind shown in the illustration. These small vessels bear a marked similarity in hull shape and rig to the contemporary working boats of the period. The sailing rig was normally a single big loose-footed mainsail and two head-sails, at first the mainsail was set with a sprit – or spreet – yard, which in the 'bezan' or leg-o'-mutton shaped sail became a long gaff, and then the familiar short curled gaff of the traditional Dutch yacht. Because of the shallow inland waters on which they were used, the *jaght*'s hull could be shallow draught, and with bluff 'apple-cheeked' bows. To correct to some extent the drift which a shallow draught sailing vessel makes to leeward, leeboards were rigged so as to counteract this and keep the boat up to windward when tacking.

The Dutch never raced their *jaghts*, preferring a kind of water-pageant, and for this it was necessary for owners to show their affluence in the riot of decoration which became so much a part of these vessels. At the time, the Dutch baroque form of decoration was a strong influence in northern Europe, and nowhere did it show itself more than in the *jaght*. Plant forms, strapping, allegorical figures, coats of arms, and grotesques were used on every possible place of vantage on exteriors and in cabins, which, supplied with leaded windows, gave light and a feeling of more space.

With modifications, the *jaght* became the English yacht as mentioned earlier. There were no royal Dutch *jaghts* as such, but William of Orange and Queen Mary used them in England.

Profile and Sail plan of a yacht built about 1670 in Amsterdam.

Exhuberantly decorated stern — Rotterdam   late 17th. Century.

R. CRABTREE

Built in Rotterdam in 1826-7, to designs by P. Glavimans Jnr. Loa 37m, beam 5·7m, draught 2m (est). Wooden hull rigged with two masts, no auxiliary sail. Engines: simple oscillating steam of 25hp, driving paddle-wheels.

In 1814, the Netherlands embarked on what was called 'an experiment in monarchy', and William I ascended the throne of an uneasy amalgam of the north and south Netherlands – then including Belgium – which lasted until 1830. From that date, with the loss of Belgium, the Dutch nation continued as a monarchy. In the days of the republic there were no royal yachts as such, but in 1827, a steam yacht was launched for the use of King William II, and once again the Dutch led the rest of Europe in having the first power yacht for a monarch.

The paddle-steamer *De Leeuw* (Lion) was an extremely modest vessel, but as can be seen in the illustration (upper), she was of sturdy construction, and followed Dutch traditions in the profusion of ornate decoration. She had a three-windowed gallery aft, and her paddle-boxes – in early steam vessels a feature of the new power – were highly decorated and resplendent with the royal Dutch arms. The tall narrow funnel – needing to be as well stayed as a mast – had a scolloped top, and from the splendid lion at the bow, the ornate gilded decoration continued aft to the windowed gallery.

During her fifty-five years of service, *De Leeuw* was often used as a tender to larger vessels. Of the many occasions when she transported the king and his family, the lower illustration shows such an event – the visit of King William II to review his fleet in Flushing Roads, 13 June 1843. The royal yacht is the white vessel left of centre – in the picture by the French artist Gudin – specially commissioned for this work. The 50 gun frigate *Rijn* is the large ship in the centre. King William II is just returning from the *Rijn* in the state barge – which can be seen passing her stern – en route for the *Leeuw* as she lies waiting to take her royal master to the shore. With the king were Princes William and Alexander, and his son-in-law the Duke of Saxe-Weinar-Eisenach.

Paddle-steamer *De Leeuw* gave long years of service, but by 1882 she was fifty-five years old, outdated and too small, so she was taken out of service and replaced by the more recently built *De Valk,* which then became the royal paddle-yacht.

Built at the Naval Dockyard in Amsterdam in 1864. Loa 250ft (est), beam 31ft (est), draught 12ft (est). Iron hull, rigged with two masts carrying steadying sail. TM tonnage: 1,042 (est). Engines: oscillating 2-cylinder, steam, working paddle-wheels, giving 12 knots (est).

The unique Dutch seaboard, with its reclaimed land, sea enclosures and network of canals, was particularly well suited for the use of paddle-wheel vessels, because – for their length – they could be of shallower draught than the screw ship. This may account for the retention of this kind of royal yacht well into a period when the screw schooner was replacing the paddle-yacht generally in Europe.

De Valk, seen in the illustration entering the harbour of Den Helder, was brought into service as the Dutch royal yacht in 1882, and

at this time was in keeping with other European royal paddle-yachts. She is flying the royal standard from her mainmast, and the occasion is an official visit of civic importance of a kind, which together with fleet reviews, kept Dutch royal yachts generally within the Netherlands. An instance of such visits was the one made by King William II, in *Leeuw*, to the Exhibition of Overijsel Industry and Art at Kempen, some fifty miles SE from the North Holland harbour of Den Helder; the year then was 1846.

King William III, who succeeded his father as King of the Netherlands in 1849, was a member of the British Royal Yacht Squadron, and *De Valk* was seen at Regatta Weeks at Cowes. The Royal Netherlands (sailing and rowing) Club was established in

1848, but on the whole Dutch kings do not seem to have participated in the more informal side of yacht racing, although Prince Hendrik, son of King William II, was held in high esteem in the marine services and patronised the sport.

During the years 1882–4, and again in 1895, *De Valk* brought members of the Royal House of the Netherlands on visits to Britain. On at least one occasion the young Princess Wilhelmina was aboard the royal paddle-yacht for such a visit. In 1890, when she succeeded her father as Queen Wilhelmina, the *De Valk* was withdrawn from service, and during the period of her reign, which saw two World Wars, and united the Dutch nation as never before under a well loved queen, no new royal yacht was commissioned to replace *De Valk*. But in the years that followed the accession of Queen Juliana, a yacht in royal ownership revived a tradition.

Piet Hein

twin-screw motor yacht

Built by N.V. Amsterdamsiber Scheeps, to designs by H. W. de Voogt in 1937, in Amsterdam. Loa 101·7ft, beam 18·7ft, draught 5ft. Steel hull. TM tonnage: 151. Engines: twin diesel, replaced in 1970 by two 6-cylinder diesels of 100 bhp, and built by the Dutch firm of DAF.

Named after a famous Dutch Admiral, *Piet Hein* is in all respects a happy royal yacht. She was built as a wedding gift for Princess (now Queen) Juliana and Prince Bernhard, and is used for pleasure on the inland waterways,

and also, in a traditional way mentioned earlier, she carries the queen on state occasions of a civic nature. The illustration of *Piet Hein* shows such an occasion, when, after the devastation of World War II, Dutch engineers had succeeded in repairing the damage, and there was the official ceremony to declare a Dutch waterway open once again.

Motor yacht *Piet Hein* is a fine example of Dutch design and building of the late 1930s. With slightly raked bow, and a sheerline broken conveniently to give good foredeck space, there is, together with the top of the deckhouse, ample room for enjoying the sun. This yacht is used only on the inland water-ways, as are a number of small motor boats owned by the royal family, but the Dutch yacht-building industry has produced. many fine seagoing motor yachts which have earned it international acclaim and trade.

The system of monarchy in the Netherlands has always been of a constitutional kind, and since the abdication of Queen Wilhelmina in favour of her daughter Juliana in 1948, it has become democratic in the modern sense. A big, seagoing official yacht would not today serve any useful purpose for the Netherlands. HRH Prince Bernhard is a keen and competent participant in a variety of sports – from skiing to piloting fast aircraft, or motor cars – but the enthusiasm for sailing is led by the queen and in particular her daughter Princess Beatrix.

Whenever a holiday from state duties can be arranged, the royal family travel to their villa at Porto Ercole in Italy, and there, in a completely informal atmosphere, they enjoy some private cruising.

HRH Princess Beatrix is much more of a devotee to yachting under sail, and her personal yacht *De Groene Draeck* is often seen, with her at the helm, in Dutch waters.

De Groene Draeck   auxiliary gaff Lemsteraak

Built by N.V. Amsterdamsibe in 1957 to designs by G. de Vries Lentsch Jnr, for HRH Princess Beatrix. Loa 49·4ft, beam 14·8ft, draught (ex lee-boards) 3·5ft. Steel hull lemsteraak. TM tonnage: 40. Engine: 6-cylinder 10 hp Perkins diesel.

Traditional working boats, particularly those used for fishing, have always influenced yacht designers, because they were developed from centuries of practical knowledge. The *Lemsteraak* stems from the sturdy fishing boats of the Friesland Islands, and thus has much common history with the first Dutch *jaght*. It is particularly fitting that a modern Dutch princess should own and personally sail a yacht which reflects these traditional qualities.

De Groene Draeck is an excellent example of what modern designers can achieve using well-tried traditional practice. Some of the early baroque decoration has been incorporated. On the big rudder-head there is a carved dragon, and, although a wheel replaces the traditional tiller, there is much carved decoration in the cockpit. The after end of the deckhouse is strikingly like earlier Dutch galleried sterns, with leaded windows and decorative carving above. The starboard window is in fact a door which leads down into the saloon. This is some 8ft by 11ft, and is completely modern in styling and furnishing, with built in settees, table and writing desk. Moving towards the bow from the saloon to starboard there is a guest cabin, shower room, and lavatory. On the port side there is a further guest cabin and a ladies' stateroom. The galley, which is forward of these, occupies the width of the yacht and is extremely well fitted. Beyond the deckhouse, under the forecastle deck, are the crew's quarters with bunks and lavatory; there is a hatch on the forecastle giving access below. All cabins have wash-basins. The engine is situated under the duckboards of the cockpit, and a 24 volt power system off the engine works lights and the necessary electric motors. Cooking is by butane gas.

The illustration shows the traditional sailing rig, big loose-footed mainsail with short curled gaff, and two headsails. At the top of her Oregon pine mast there is a curiously carved finial, possibly a reminder that this rig may have originally come to Holland from the East Indies. On a wind, with her leeboard down and the carved sun and stars at her bluff bows taking the spray, *Groene Draeck* is a fine sight. More often than not, Princess Beatrix is at the helm of this tradition-linking royal yacht.

Norge

twin-screw motor yacht

Built by Camper & Nicholsons in 1937 at Southampton. Loa 263ft, beam 38ft, draught 14·5ft. Steel hull rigged with two masts. TM tonnage: 1,611. Engines: two MAN 8-cylinder diesels, giving 3,000 bhp, and a cruising speed of 14 knots. Originally named Philante.

Norway, like her Scandinavian neighbours, has two histories. One stretches back into the dim past to the days of high-prowed boats of men who were already the ancestors of the Vikings. Her modern history really starts in 1814, when she gained her independence after 500 years of Danish rule, and elected to be united with Sweden under Carl XIII. But in 1905 Norway gained her complete independence, and became a separate kingdom. For their monarch the Norwegians chose the Danish Prince Carl who had married Maud, the daughter of the British King Edward VII. He assumed the title of Haakon VII and ruled by his motto 'All for Norway' with distinction and popularity until his death in 1957.

The fact that the Norwegian nation bought the big motor yacht *Philante* from Britain where, during World War II she had been in the service of the Royal Navy, refitting her as the Royal Norwegian Yacht *Norge*, was a high tribute to their king who with his son, Crown Prince Olaf, had inspired the nation to resist aggression, and to fight on from Britain after 1940. *Norge*, in 1947, was the biggest and most impressive royal yacht in Europe. Built by Camper & Nicholsons for T. O. M. Sopwith, she was the biggest motor yacht built in Britain, and was fitted out like a small luxury cruise liner. With owner's suite and eight guest cabins, five saloons and the most elaborately equipped galley of any yacht, she was certainly fit for a king – and still is, being in commission today for use by HM King Olaf.

Informal sailing and racing has long been a royal activity in Norway. The Royal Norwegian Sailing Club, established in 1883, has the king's patronage, and he is a member of the RYS, owning at the moment the 8 metre *Sira*, and the two 5·5 metres *Norna* and *Bingo*. HRH Crown Prince Harald has owned six yachts from the $12\frac{1}{2}$ kvm, to his latest 'Soling' sloop – all consecutively named *Fram*. HRH Crown Princess Sonja has owned two 'Yngling' class yachts – *Flaks* and *Flaks II*, and Princesses Astrid and Ragnhild jointly own the $12\frac{1}{2}$ kvm *Astra*. Off the shores of Ostfold in Oslo fjord, on the island of Hanko, King Olaf has a summer villa, and from here he can watch international yachts racing at what has deservedly become known as the 'Cowes of the North'.

PORTUGAL

Amelia II

Built by Ramage & Ferguson of Leith in 1880, and originally called Fair Geraldine *and then* Geraldine. *Loa 148ft, beam 21·1ft, draught 11·1ft. Iron hull rigged as a three-masted topsail schooner. TM tonnage: 301. Engines: compound steam, 2-cylinder inverted, 55 hp; built by Walker Henderson & Co, Scotland.*

Portugal has been called an Atlantic-facing coastal strip of Europe, and it was her geographical position which sent her people south and west across the ocean in search of new lands and fortunes. From the fifteenth century, King Henry the Navigator, and such men as Magellan and Vasco da Gama, established Portugal as the greatest trading nation in Europe, whose newly discovered sea routes to the Indies had at last broken the Levantine stranglehold, and whose colonies were extensive and productive. However, her commitments became unmanageable, and decline soon overtook success.

Shipbuilding expertise, Portugal's early heritage, provided her monarchs with splendid royal barges, but, it was not until the nineteenth century that royal yachts appeared in the great harbour of Lisbon, and King Carlos owned the modest 147 ton steam yacht *Amelia*, the first of three of that name. The illustration is of the second *Amelia*, and it can be seen that she was not only a fine example of the skill of Ramage & Ferguson, but also a typical steam yacht of the period when steam and sail were of equal importance in one hull.

King Carlos I who succeeded Luis I as King of Portugal in 1889, seems to have been keenly interested in steam yachts since he owned not only the three *Amelia*s, but also the *Yacoma* of 635 tons, and the small 56 ton *Sado*. But *Amelia II* was his favourite, judging by the many sketches and paintings the king – a competent artist – made of her, and which are in the *Album of 1899*, published by the Fundacao da Casa de Breganca in Portugal.

There is also the *Amelia*'s diary in the Vasco da Gama Maritime Museum, which contains sketches.

The Real Associacoa Naval Lisboa, established in 1856, was matched in 1891 by a yacht club, of a kind imperative to the climate of fashionable royalty of that period – the Real Club Naval de Lisboa. King Carlos was commodore of both these establishments. and his queen and the dowager queen were both keen sailing yachtswomen.

Amelia III

Built by Ramage & Ferguson at Leith in 1900, to designs by Cox & King. Loa 229·5ft, beam 29·5ft, draught 10·5ft. Steel hull rigged with two masts. TM tonnage: 899. Engines: two triple-expansion 6-cylinder steam, fed by two Scotch boilers, giving 386 nhp. Originally named Banshee.

Colonel Harry MacCalmont, an extremely wealthy, and enthusiastic equestrian and yachtsman, could be said to have supplied two monarchies with royal yachts. He had built the earlier steam yacht *Giralda* which finally became the Spanish royal yacht (see p83), and the *Amelia* was originally built as the *Banshee* and in his ownership. On his death the yacht was sold to the Portuguese Government, renamed *Amelia* and entered service as the royal yacht in 1904.

The third *Amelia* was very much the maverick of the trio of that name, and although from a famous yacht-yard, and designed by the distinguished firm of Cox & King, she has very little of the look of the contemporary steam yacht. The 'ram' bow – the reverse in rake of the 'clipper' bow – and her tall narrow funnels, give her much more the appearance of a small warship of the period. It is possible that the Portuguese may have had this in mind,

as an alternative to her role as royal yacht, when they bought the *Banshee*.

It is hoped that in the four years preceding his assassination, King Carlos was often able to use the newly acquired *Amelia*, and to gain occasional respite from the cares of the Portuguese crown which were steadily mounting against him. She must have been a fast, handy vessel, with comfortable and well fitted accommodation. In 1910, when the republic had been proclaimed in Portugal, *Amelia*, serving for the last time as a royal yacht, steamed into Gibraltar harbour carrying into exile the Portuguese royal family.

With her name changed again, this time to *Cinco du Octoubro*, the ex-royal yacht became in 1911, a despatch vessel – that vague category into which many royal yachts seem, at some time, to have been placed – but later did excellent work and much sea-time as the official Portuguese survey ship. Finally, in 1936, this elderly steam yacht was again re-classified and entered the Portuguese navy as a gunboat armed with two 47mm guns.

No evidence is available to tell how the steam yacht which looked like a gunboat actually performed when she was a gunboat; but significantly she does not appear after 1937.

Amelia III

ROMANIA

Luceafarul

Built by John Brown Ltd, on the Clyde, to designs by G. L. Watson & Co, in 1930. Loa 300ft, beam 36ft, draught 14·8ft. Steel hull rigged with two masts. TM tonnage: 1,574. Engines: two geared steam turbines, fed by two water-tube boilers, oil fired, giving 4,000 bhp and a speed of 17·4 knots. Originally named Nahlin.

A prevailing attitude among the national statesmen of many of the nineteenth-century Balkan kingdoms seems to have been that it was better to have an imported royal dynasty, than one chosen from a continually feud-torn indigenous upper class. In 1881, Romania received as the first king of her independent state, the Hohenzollern prince, who became Charles I. The infusion of the rigid formalism of the Prussian court with the romantic and colourful exhuberance of the Romanian people, produced a Ruritanian court prototype, which has fed the pages of western writers and operettas from Anthony Hope to Ivor Novello. The final scenes of royal Romania were played out between the wars, with, as the principal actors, the beautiful, but unorthodox Dowager Queen Marie, and the scandalous, but handsome King Carol – the last monarch to rule Romania – who came to the throne dramatically

from self-imposed exile in 1930, and departed into exile for good in 1940.

Although the Romanian royal family may have seemed somewhat bizarre in their general behaviour, they also had a sporting side which had been fostered by Queen Marie – herself an extremely keen and able horsewoman – and yachting from Constanza and the Black Sea resorts was encouraged. Princess Ileana, who owned the 12 ton auxiliary ketch *Isprava* (originally built by Thornycrofts as *Mookerjee*) qualified for her Yachtmaster's Certificate in 1928. Of official royal yachts, the elderly paddle-yacht *Stefan Cel Mare* – originally built at Budapest as the *Orient* in 1870 – did service on the Danube. But in King Carol's reign a yacht of quality was acquired.

The scandalous behaviour of King Carol became world news in the 1930s, and the name of his mistress, Helen Lepescu is still associated with the downfall of this rather tragic royal misfit. But it was she who persuaded him to purchase the steam yacht *Nahlin*, which was renamed *Luceafarul*, because she was intrigued by the romantic part this yacht had played in the lives of the Duke of Windsor and Mrs Simpson. This splendid vessel – one of the last of her kind – had spacious and beautifully appointed accommodation. Her original owner, Lady Yule, had roamed the world in her, but as the Romanian royal yacht she made but one cruise in the Aegean. Renamed as *Liberatatea*, this magnificent yacht now serves the Romanian Republic.

IMPERIAL RUSSIA

Livadia

triple-screw steam yacht

Built by John Elder & Co of Govan, in 1880 to plans supplied by the Imperial Russian Admiralty. Loa 266ft, beam 153ft, draught 6·5ft. Steel hull of unorthodox eliptical plan, and rig. TM tonnage: 11,802. Engines: three sets of compound two stage expansion steam, fed by eight in-line-athwartships boilers, producing 10,500 ihp, and a speed of 15·9 knots.

The voyage which, in 1697, Peter the Great undertook and which led him to the capitals of Europe, is seen by historians as the beginning of the process of westernisation by which this early Romanov tsar started a barbarous and backward country on the ladder to civilisation. He was anxious and quick to learn from all he saw abroad. Perhaps his greatest lessons were learnt in England, where, at Deptford, spellbound at the uninhibited and coarse behaviour of the Muscovy tsar and his courtiers, the tradesmen of the royal dockyards yielded the secrets of their crafts.

In the Baltic Fleet, and the reorganised Russian Army, were to be seen the fruits of Peter the Great's determination to make his country powerful in Europe at a time when most of that continent saw her as wholly Asiatic. It has been claimed that Peter I was also responsible for introducing yachting into Russia; but what is described as such, is not much more than a further manifestation of the wild and irresponsible attitude of the tsar to his courtiers – admittedly a strange assortment – and there was certainly no pleasure involved in the kind of horse-play which went on in boats on the Neva River.

By the nineteenth century, the Romanov dynasty was reaching its zenith as a supremely autocratic regime, whose empire stretched from the Baltic to the Pacific, and from the Arctic Circle to the Black Sea. The advent of the steam yacht gave yet another chance to show the bottomless purse of imperial noblesse.

The *Livadia* was the most spectacular of all the Romanov steam yachts.

This extraordinary vessel was elliptical in shape. A turbot-like lower hull provided buoyancy and the space for the engines, boilers, and working room, as well as having a double bottom subdivided into watertight compartments. The upper hull was more conventionally shaped and provided the necessary accommodation for a very large ship's company, and the imperial suite, which occupied the whole of the upper and shelter deck area. The illustration gives an idea of the spectacle of *Livadia* at sea.

Livadia

interior of imperial dining-room

The design of *Livadia* came from original ideas – so prevalent in the nineteenth century – for a circular ship, produced by John Elder of Glasgow. Russian Admiral Popov used the idea in several floating gun-platforms, circular in shape and propelled by six screws placed athwartships at one 'end'. These 'Popovkas' – as they were called – gave rise to the more elliptical design of *Livadia* when she was ordered for Tsar Alexander II in 1880. The whole conception was to be, literally, a floating palace for the imperial use on the shallow waters of the Black Sea. She suffered a great deal from 'slamming' during her trip across

the Bay of Biscay, and was forced to lay up in the Spanish port of El Ferrol, where only temporary repairs could be effected; she finally arrived in Sevastopol, ironically, after Alexander II had been assassinated.

In the illustration of the imperial dining-room, can be seen the idiom of grandeur and shore-side magnificence which permeated the whole of the imperial accommodation. With *Livadia*'s enormous beam of 153ft, and the fact that the deckhouse constructions on two decks gave 12ft headroom, there could be installed all the accoutrements of a royal palace in the Romanov style. This was done in furnishing and decoration in a traditional Byzantine flavoured Victorianism – a mixture of the exotic with western urbanity – reflected in many of the large country houses belonging to the imperial family, and the aristocratic circles of the Russian social hierarchy in the late nineteenth century.

The imperial dining-room was outdone in luxurious splendour by the Grand Salon, in which there was a fountain surrounded by flower beds! Throughout the imperial suite, corridor floors were finished in marble mosaics. All this very non-maritime equipment and the overall conception of *Livadia* was based on the assumption that her design would eradicate undue movement and in particular rolling, to which motion steam yachts were very prone until the roll stabiliser was perfected late in the present century. *Livadia* did not entirely vindicate her design, but in the Black Sea she was remarkably steady.

It seems that the most unusual royal yacht ever built was not used by the imperial family. A new steam yacht was built in 1888, and after repairing the damage she had suffered crossing the Bay of Biscay in the vast dry-dock used for the 'Popovkas', *Livadia* stayed in Sevastopol until broken up in 1926.

Poliarnaia Zvesda

twin-screw schooner

Built in St Petersburg in 1888, by the Baltiiski Shipbuilding Co. Loa 336·5ft, beam 46ft, draught 15ft (est). Steel hull rigged with three masts. TM tonnage: 3,270. Engines: two 6-cylinder compound steam, fed by ten boilers, producing 7,496 hp. Engines also built by Baltiiski.

Alexander III, the penultimate Romanov tsar, succeeded to the imperial throne in 1881, following the tragic assassination of his father. He at once showed that there was to be no watering down of autocratic rule by an infusion of liberalism or the granting of a constitution. For thirteen years the great Russian Empire continued, ostensibly, in the traditions of conservatism and status quo.

Steam yacht *Poliarnaia Zvesda* – 'Pole Star' – was by 1889 the official imperial yacht, and as can be seen from the illustration – as smoke from her saluting guns momentarily obscures her forecastle – built and engined by Russian craftsmen, she was a fine big steam yacht of a design much in keeping with contemporary European styles. She has perhaps a greater look of aggressive purpose about her that was lacking in the Clyde-built steam yacht of the period.

Poliarnaia Zvesda served her imperial owner well. During Alexander III's reign, the elaborate security arrangements which were necessary to ensure that the son did not meet the father's tragic end, meant that the tsar's movements became more and more limited to a strict schedule in the company of his Empress Marie Fedorovna and their five children. The highlight of the year for them all was their return each summer to the imperial residence at Peterhof, and from here there were pleasant areas conveniently near. The most relaxing of

all their activities was the annual cruise in the Baltic aboard *Poliarnaia Zvesda*.

The cruise usually included a visit to the Swedish royal family at their summer residence on the Baltic, and it was here, off the coast, on these occasions that a family gathering of royal yachts took place. It was a delight to young and old, with accommodation in the royal palace ashore bursting at the seams, and the children housed in chalets in the grounds of the palace.

Such occasions, and particularly whilst aboard the yacht, provided Alexander III with the few chances to relax with his family, and to forget for the moment the nagging fear of an assassin's bomb or bullet.

Standart

Built by Burmeister & Wain in Copenhagen in 1895. Loa 420ft, beam 50·4ft, draught 20ft. Steel hull rigged with three masts. TM tonnage: 4,334. Engines: two triple-expansion 6-cylinder steam (built by Burmeister & Wain), fed by twenty-four Belleville boilers, giving 10,600 ihp, and a speed of 18 knots.

At the accession of Tsar Nicholas II, following the death (from natural causes) of his father, the scene was set for the playing out of the years that ended in the brutal murder of the tsar and his family and the fury of the revolution. In 1894, however, although the new tsar was deemed to be altogether too ineffectual to be an autocrat, the all important status quo appeared to be maintained. Also in this year, the *Poliarnaia Zvesda* was engaged in a romantic voyage to England carrying Nicholas II to plight his troth to Princess Alix of Hesse-Darmstadt – a granddaughter of Queen Victoria – who became his Empress Alexandra Fedorovna.

When *Standart* was commissioned she was the biggest and most impressive royal yacht in Europe at the time, and in Russia the gay and fashionable life of the court and some forty grand dukes and duchesses continued unabated. There were then many yacht clubs for the

élite from the Baltic to the Black Sea, led by the St Petersburg Imperial, established in 1846.

The new imperial yacht was superbly equipped. Apart from the usual state rooms and saloons, there was a chapel, and children's room; and the upper deck was arranged so that the imperial family could use it almost completely as a promenade, or for games and alfresco meals.

With a carefully selected company of officers and men, the latter often being entrusted with the children, Nicholas and his family regarded *Standart*, and the now less-used *Poliarnaia Zvesda*, as a veritable refuge from the sinister events which began to overtake them. But *Standart* was also very much used for formal occasions, such as the departure of the ill-fated Russian Fleet in the Japanese War, the reception of European diplomats, or meetings with the German Kaiser, as well as the many visits to Cowes Week Regattas, at one of which the tsar had reviewed the British Fleet.

After the gruesome murder of the imperial family, when the fire of revolution swept Russia, *Poliarnaia Zvesda* is recorded as having had her stokers' quarters used to imprison the tsarina's confidante Anna Vyrubova. *Standart* emerged to serve in the Soviet Navy as the minelayer *Marti* until the 1960s.

SPAIN

Giralda

twin-screw schooner

*Built in 1894 by Fairfield Shipbuilding &
Engineering Co, of Glasgow. Loa 289ft, beam
35·1ft, draught 12ft (est). Steel hull rigged with
three masts. TM tonnage: 1,664. Engines: two
triple-expansion 6-cylinder steam, fed by five
boilers, producing 420 nhp, and a speed of
20·5 knots.*

In the sixteenth century, with successive
monarchs dedicated to the religious sub-
jugation of Europe, and vast colonies acquired
in the New World, Spain was at the height
of her power, as was her navy. But with the
Mediterranean and Atlantic seas to control,
and with sea warfare requiring a different kind
of ship in each, Spain did not accommodate
her shipbuilding to this fact. When her
colonies became unmanageable, the home
country suffered and the decline set in.

There had been royal ships and barges of
magnificence, but until the accession of King
Alphonso XIII in 1902, there had been little
of what had then become fashionable yachting.
However, when he came to the throne, there
already existed in the Spanish Navy a steam
yacht of size and distinction – the *Giralda* –
bought by Spain at the time of the American
War, from the wealthy yachtsman Colonel
MacCalmont in 1898. She had been used as a

despatch vessel, and in her the young Alphonso had already made cruises off the Spanish coast.

When he became king she was used a great deal by him, and as he was a member of the British Royal Yacht Squadron, she was often seen at Cowes Week Regattas.

Steam yacht *Giralda* was by way of being something of a phenomenon in the yachting world of the 1890s. In her design, Cox & King, and Fairfields set a pattern which they followed in later building – the built up forecastle with an almost straight sheer from the break right aft, comparatively low freeboard, centre line deckhouses, big funnel with its top parallel to the waterline, and an elliptical counter stern. *Giralda* was also the first private yacht to exceed 1,000 tons. Her interior accommodation was exceptionally well fitted out and spacious. Everything about her, not least her powerful engines – also built by Fairfields – set new standards which influenced steam yacht design.

King Alphonso must have delighted in this elegant yacht, seen to advantage among the assembled royal yachts on occasions at Cowes. After his abdication, and the declaration of the Spanish Republic, *Giralda* served in the Spanish Navy as a survey vessel, and does not appear listed after 1935.

Tonino

cutter: International Class 10 metre

Designed by W. Fife, and built by Astilleros del Nervion in 1911 at Bilbao, Spain. Loa 43·75ft, beam 9·34ft, draught 6·3ft. Wooden hull rigged as gaff topsail cutter; sail area 1,850sq ft. Sails by Ratsey & Lapthorn. TM tonnage: 16.

The sight of King Alphonso's cutter *Torino* (sail number FO) as she fights it out with *Irex* on a reach off the Isle of Wight, is a reminder of the sort of racing yachts that made their

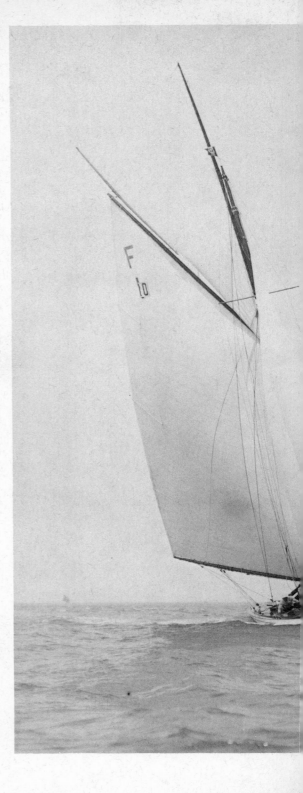

appearance in an attempt by yachtsmen to have boats that could, as near as possible, race as equals. They were known as the 'Metre Boats', and ranged from the big 15 metres of which the King of Spain owned the *Hispania*, to the smaller 6 metre class. In the latter he owned *Barandil*, with *Tonino* falling between the two.

King Alphonso rarely missed a Regatta Week at Cowes. As a friend (and relative, as he had married his niece) of King Edward VII, and a member of the RYS, he was well known as a great sportsman who delighted in sailing his yachts hard, and had a friendly and appreciative eye for other people's craft. In *Tonino* and the king's other yachts everything was of the best at a time when superlative natural materials were available, and the resultant yachts were a delight to see. The gaff topsail cutter, stemming from the older working boat rig of running bowsprit and jackyard topsail over a loose-footed big mainsail, was a particularly splendid sight in a smart breeze.

The last Spanish king was an enthusiast for many sports as well as for yachting. His keenness on the fast motor cars of the period may have accounted for his ownership of an early motor yacht – the *Fackung-Tu-Zinc* – which was built for him in 1913 by S. E. Saunders Ltd, of Cowes. She was 50ft long and 16 tons, and her twin screws were driven by two pioneer Hispania Suiza 8-cylinder petrol engines.

In 1931, King Alphonso XIII abdicated in favour of the short-lived republic which was supplanted by the present Franco regime in Spain. During his reign which saw in Europe many changes in royal yachting, and particularly in the design of the yachts themselves, the king was a supporter of innovations which were for the good of the sport as a whole. In this way, like that followed by both the British Kings Edward VII and George V, royal patronage and knowledgeable enthusiasm secured the healthy development of international yacht racing.

SWEDEN

Amphion

Built in Stockholm in 1778 to designs of F. H. Chapman. Loa 160ft (est), and of shallow draught. For the use of King Gustav III, especially for cruising on Lake Malaren and in the Finnish Archipelago.

Traditionally, Sweden has continually been aware of Russian moves towards the Baltic, which cost her an earlier empire after her defeat of 1708. From that date Swedish history follows a similar pattern to that of Denmark, in which Norway, until 1905, was used as a territorial incentive to alliance and the balance of power. The accession of Gustav III as king in 1771 brought to Sweden an age of autocratic monarchy, and also a cultural renaissance which grew with successive generations and moved Sweden into the nineteenth century as a modern industrially developing nation.

Royal yachts in Sweden have not always been of the official or specific kind. The *Amphion* is the best of earlier examples; interesting because of her design and rig – which included the use of oars, with a canvas waist-cloth amidships that was raised when the oars were to be used. As one of a number of British craftsmen working generally in Scandinavia in the eighteenth century, F. H. Chapman was noted for a type of shallow draught frigate used by the Swedish Navy,

but *Amphion* has been termed a schooner although topsails on both masts were rarely seen after the end of the eighteenth century. His ideas of combining shallow draught with greater speed tended to make his schooners 'cranky' and unsuitable for use in the open sea.

Amphion was built expressly as a pleasure yacht for King Gustav III, and as such was used on festive and ceremonial occasions, and for cruising among the islands of the Finnish archipelago. By all accounts she was fitted out with spacious and luxurious accommodation for the king and queen and their suite. Both the interior, and exterior decoration was rendered in what is known as the Swedish 'Gustavian' classical style – similar in basic conception to the neo-classical styles appearing generally in Europe in the eighteenth century. Chapman himself is thought to have been responsible for the overall scheme of decoration for *Amphion*, but the splendid sculpture and relief decoration on the stern, and the figure-head was the work of the Swedish sculptor Per Ljung.

Amphion saw moments of dramatic action. During the Russian War of 1788–90 she served as royal headquarters. On King Gustav III's death in 1792, she became a depot ship until broken up in 1885.

Drott

screw schooner

Built at Stockholm by Bergsunds Mekaniska Verstad, in 1877 – originally named Ran. *Loa 175ft, beam 27ft (est), draught 11·5ft (est). TM tonnage: 630. Engines: compound steam engines driving a single screw (est) giving 12 knots. Iron hull (est) rigged with two masts.*

From 1883, the steam yacht *Ran* was renamed *Drott* and became the royal yacht of King Oscar II. She represents a very different phase in Sweden's history, from the days of *Amphion*. The reign of King Oscar I had seen a great liberalisation of Swedish life and political outlook. On the accession to the throne in 1872 of King Oscar II, Sweden was set fair on the path of neutrality in European wars, industrialisation, and the particular brand of democratic monarchy which she has since followed.

Drott is an interesting example of Swedish shipbuilding. At a time when British steam yachts were following the handsome lines of the clipper hull, she has an unmistakable look of what was some thirty years later in Britain to be incorporated into the new motor yacht design – the steam trawler. The long gentle sheer almost straight stem, and overhang counter, give *Drott* a powerful but elegant appearance. Her narrow funnels, well raked with her masts give her a purposeful look despite her somewhat modest size.

The reign of King Oscar II (1872–1907), was a period in which Europe's royalty was intent on impressive displays of regal prestige, displays however which were not inherent to the Swedish monarchy, and which therefore did not see the replacing of *Drott* by a larger and more luxurious vessel. The king was a member of the Royal Yacht Squadron, but from contemporary accounts he does not seem to have used *Drott* for his visits to Cowes Week Regattas. In fact, Julius Gabe, in his book *Yachting*, published in 1902 is somewhat scathing about the King of Sweden who 'has only a few sailing craft none over 50 tons'. This suggests that King Oscar II used during Cowes Week the sailing yachts *Mathilda* (25 tons), *Max* (22 tons), and the *Vanadis* (40 tons), all of which were on the establishment of the Swedish Navy.

Swedish monarchs have reflected their

nation's great seafaring traditions by their encouragement of private yachting, particularly in the Baltic. As early as 1832 the Royal Swedish Yacht Club was founded under the patronage of King Charles XIV. Since that time informal sail racing and cruising have become the forms of yachting in which monarch and subjects find a common heritage and delight.

Erthogroul

twin-screw schooner

Built by Sir W. G. Armstrong Whitworth & Co Ltd, at Newcastle-on-Tyne in 1904, to designs by J. R. Perrett. Loa 264ft, beam 27·7ft, draught 14ft. Steel hull rigged with three masts. TM tonnage: 964. Engines: two triple-expansion 6-cylinder steam, of 144 nhp, driving twin-screws. Built by Hawthorn, Leslie & Co, of Newcastle.

The name of this steam yacht of a twentieth-century Turkish sultan honoured a national hero – Erthogroul. His son, Osman, in 1290, led his tribe of vigorous, hard-working nomad Turks, in a continuous movement of absorption and conquest towards the West. In two centuries, the Osmanlis had captured Constantinople and much of the decaying Byzantine Empire, incorporating Greek culture and ideas in the process. Under Suleiman the Magnificent, in 1529, the Turks reached the gates of Vienna, from which, however, they were turned back; the Ottoman Empire had then achieved its peak.

Turkish naval power dominated the Mediterranean until the defeat at Lepanto in 1571, when it then ruled the eastern end of that sea. But in this period, the sultans' royal ships and barges were of an unequalled magnificence. The decadence of the Ottoman Empire in the nineteenth century made it the 'sick man of Europe' – unable fully to integrate western ideas with Islamic ideals – but, like most other European fashions, the nineteenth-century steam yacht was accepted. In 1898 the *Teshrifiyeh*, of single-screw, 78 TM tons, and Turkish built, was commissioned for the use of Sultan Abdul Hamid; it was then followed by the screw barge *Seughudlu*, in 1903, and in the next year *Erthogroul* – both built by Armstrong Whitworths.

The *Erthogroul* continued in use by Mohammed V, sultan in 1909, who, ruling until 1918, was virtually the last Turkish emperor. This fine vessel, was clearly a large, elegant yacht. The sizeable structure abaft the mizzen mast on the shelter deck, with its close-fitting awning, probably housed the Saraglio. The traditional aura of sublimity which surrounded the sultans makes it unlikely that there was any informal royal yachting, and the Prinkipio Yacht Club, established in 1898 at Constantinople, with Sir Edwin Pears as President, does not seem to have had imperial patronage.

Ironically, it was the President of the Turkish Republic who, in 1938, was given the *Savarona* – the largest private steam yacht ever built!

YUGOSLAVIA

Dubrovnik torpedo boat destroyer

Built on the Clyde in 1931 by Messrs Yarrow. Loa 371·5ft, beam 35ft, draught 11·7ft. Standard displacement 1,880 tons. Engines: Parsons geared turbines, fed by three Yarrow boilers, producing 42,000 bhp, and a speed of 37 knots. Built for the Royal Yugoslavian Navy, and specifically designed to be an economical and fast steamer.

After the collapse of Turkish rule and the end of Austro-Hungarian influence in 1918, the kingdom of Yugoslavia emerged as a potentially explosive mixture of Serb and Croat national aspirations. From 1921, the reins of government were largely in the hands of King Alexander I – called the 'strong man of the Balkans' – who, as the last of the line of 'peasant kings' – the Karageorges – ruled the newly formed kingdom autocratically but wisely.

The pride of the Yugoslavian Navy was the destroyer *Dubrovnik*. In 1932, this fine ship formed the core of a small fleet of which she was the largest unit, and although, as a warship, she could not be classed as a yacht, nevertheless she took on the duties of an official royal yacht for King Alexander and his family. Her after accommodation was arranged so as to provide quarters for the king and queen and their suite when required. The *Dubrovnik* was used for official visits to Bulgaria and Turkey in 1933, but for shorter journeys and cruises for relaxation, there were two other royal yachts on the navy's establishment. These were the *Dragor* – 250 ton paddle-vessel, ex-Austrian river patrol boat – and the older screw yacht *Vila* of 230 tons. The *Dragor* was used exclusively on the Danube – the ancient 'Amber Route' which serves the Balkans, and *Vila* was used for cruising down through the Dalmatian Islands.

It is certain that yachts have always provided a refuge for royalty from the cares of state and crown, in the case of Alexander of Yugoslavia these became increasingly linked with assassination, threats and attempts increasingly emanating from dissident Croat extremists aided and abetted by Mussolini for his own political ends. In 1934 this evil group achieved its goal.

On an official visit to France in October of that year, the King left Yugoslavia in the *Dubrovnik*. The two days which he spent at sea were to be his last. On the morning of 9 October, King Alexander I of Yugoslavia was shot and killed by fanatics as he drove in state from the harbour of Marseilles. This tragedy brought the regency of Prince Paul, but World War II saw the end of monarchy in Yugoslavia.

ACKNOWLEDGEMENTS

I should like to thank the London embassies of the nations represented in this book for their advice and help leading to information from their respective countries. Of the many national institutions in Europe and Britain, from which I have had generous help, my special thanks are due to the directors and staffs of the following: the Institut Belge, Exterior Relations Division, Brussels; the Orlogsmuseet, Copenhagen; the Fundacao da Casa de Breganca, Lisbon; Imperial War Museum, and Science Museum, London; the Department of Naval History, Royal Netherlands Navy; the Kongelig Norsk Seilforening and Norinform, Oslo; the Museé de la Marine, Paris; Historical Section of the Italian Navy, Rome; Staens Sjöhistoriska Museum, Stockholm; the Austrian Heeresgeschichtliches Museum, and the Staatsarchiv-Kriegsarchiv, Vienna; and also to the chief archivist of the royal palace, Brussels, the archivist of the royal palace, Monaco and the ADC to His Royal Highness the Prince of the Netherlands.

My gratitude is particularly due to the librarians of: Taunton; Somerset County, especially Bridgwater and the Bishops Lydeard branch; Naval History Department of Plymouth Central; and the National Maritime Museum Library, London.

For much general help I am indebted to my wife, and to Mrs Judith Bird, R. G. Dickens and D. J. Mills.

R.C.

ILLUSTRATIONS

The plates in this volume are reproduced by courtesy of the following:

Beken of Cowes for *Ul*, *Britannia*, *Britannia and Coweslip*, *Hohenzollern*, *Meteor IV*, *Princesse Alice*, *Norge*, *Luceafarul*, *Standart*, and *Tonino*.

Department of Naval History, Royal Netherlands Navy for *De Leeuw*, and *De Valk*.

Historical Section, Italian Navy, Rome for *Savoia I*, *Trinacria*, and *Savoia II*.

Imperial War Museum for *Victoria and Albert III* (interior), *Grille*, *Poliarnaia Zvesda*, and *Giralda*.

Institut Belge, Brussels for *Alberta*.

Maritime Photo Library, Cromer for *Dannebrog* (screw schooner).

Messrs Yarrow Ltd, Glasgow for *Dubrovnik*.

Musée de la Marine, Paris for the Versailles flotilla, *Le Canot Impérial*, *L'Aigle*, *Jérôme Napoléon*, and *La Reine Hortense*.

Nationaal Foto-Persbureau NV, Amsterdam for *Piet Hein*, and *De Groene Draeck*.

Orlogsmuseet, Copenhagen for *Elephanten*, *Slesvig*, and *Dannebrog* (paddle-schooner).

Osterreichisches Staatsarchiv-Kriegsarchiv, Vienna for *Fantasie*, and *Miramar*.

Radio Times Hulton Picture Library for the Dragon Class yacht.

Science Museum, London for *Safa-El-Bahr*, and *Lividia* (interior).

Statens Sjöhistoriska Museum, Stockholm for *Drott*.

Illustrations not acknowledged above are by the author: *Fubbs*, *Royal George*, *Victoria and Albert I–III*, *Nadiejda*, *Mahroussa* and *Kassed Kheir*, *Kaiseradler*, the Dutch jaght, *Amelia II and III*, *Livadia*, *Amphion*, and *Erthogroul*.

In the production of these, reference has been made to photographs, contemporary marine paintings and other material originating from sources in the National Maritime Museum, London; the Nederlandsh Historisch Scheepvaart Museum, Amsterdam; Statens Sjöhistoriska Museum, Stockholm; and *Jane's Fighting Ships*.